T0209463

"Dr. Eves has written an insightful and visionary book to inspire and encourage preachers to take seriously the task of biblical preaching as it relates to the need for apologetic messages from the pulpit in the 21st century."

- **Dr. E. E. Elliott, PhD, M. Div.**
Department Chair of Biblical Leadership and Ministry,
Director of Pulpit Communication and Expository Preaching
at Trinity College of the Bible and Theological Seminary

"Dr. Eves gives a compelling call for preachers to engage their congregations with the Word of God in such a way as to touch their heads, their hearts, and their hands. This is accomplished by being true to the context of the Scriptures, by the use of carefully crafted rhetoric designed to convince and convict, and by addressing the special concerns of a postmodern congregation. Dr. Eves calls upon the testimony of a wide variety of Christian scholars, both ancient and contemporary, as well as on his own experience as a university professor to call us to this threefold path. In addressing these concerns, he gives us an apologetic for apologetics, showing the need for providing real reasons in support of faith. He then calls for expository preaching as a means to proclaiming the gospel as the central message of Christianity."

-**John T. Stevenson, D.Min.**,
Professor at South Florida Bible College & Theological Seminary

"The Postmodern movement is a great threat to the Christian Church and is pointed at undermining the message of the Bible. In view of the current attack on the Bible, the serious Christian must know how to defend what they believe. This in-depth study on Apologetics and Rhetoric will enable both the preacher and the man in the pew to effectively challenge, debate, and win the argument."

-**Rev. Ralph D. Curtin, D. Min**.
Pastor and Author

Apologetics and Rhetoric:

The Right Combination for Expositor Preaching to a Postmodern World

John Cameron Eves PhD, DRS

WESTBOW
PRESS®
A DIVISION OF THOMAS NELSON
& ZONDERVAN

WestBow Press books may be ordered through booksellers or by contacting:

WestBow Press
A Division of Thomas Nelson & Zondervan
1663 Liberty Drive
Bloomington, IN 47403
www.westbowpress.com
1 (866) 928-1240

ISBN: 978-1-9736-7106-0 (sc)
ISBN: 978-1-9736-7105-3 (hc)
ISBN: 978-1-9736-7107-7 (e)

Library of Congress Control Number: 2019910920

Print information available on the last page.

WestBow Press rev. date: 8/7/2019

Contents

Acknowledgements

To my wife, Grace, who has stood by me throughout my years of study. She not only supported me in the writing of this book but also encouraged me to make this possible.

To my sons, Eric and Isaac, whom I am so proud of. I thank them for all their help and support not just with this book but also for all their help and support throughout the years.

I wish to express my sincere gratitude to all who contributed to this publication. At Trinity International University I earned a B.A. in Biblical Studies and a Masters in Religion. It was there that I established a sound solid Biblical foundation as I sat under such Professors as Dr. Gary Cohen and other academics.

At Trinity Theological Seminary, I continued my studies and earned a Doctorate of Religious Studies in the area of Expository Preaching, as I sat under Dr. E.E. Elliott who taught me how to present the Word of God.

In addition, I graduated with a Ph.D. in Christian Apologetics at Trinity Theological Seminary under the direction of Dr. Braxton Hunter where the primary concentration was on defending the faith by means of logic and reason.

Most of all, I thank Christ for everything. Without Him, I would have nothing.

Foreword

I've read a lot of books about preaching throughout my 40-plus years as a pastor and national church leader in the Pentecostal Assemblies of Canada and during my 13 years as Editor of *Testimony*, the official publication of the aforementioned body. Some I read for curiosity, others to review in various publications, and some, like Apologetics and Rhetoric: *The Right Combination for Preaching to a Post Modern World* by Dr. John Eves, I read for pure enjoyment.

Dr. Eves has done young preachers a huge service by mapping out a sound and thoroughly biblical strategy for reaching the current world. In case you were tempted to sideline this book thinking that there are more pressing needs demanding your attention, I would point out the importance of the single preposition "to" in the subtitle.

Many modern Christian apologists alert us to the fact that we live *"in"* a post modern world and therefore, need to find a way to engage with the postmodern listener, if indeed, you are fortunate enough to find them among your audience on any given Sunday. Dr. Eves, on the other hand, gives us a blueprint for preaching *"to"* the postmodernist who will surely be among your audience. This simple prepositional detail is of ultimate importance if we are to remain relevant to our culture yet faithful to our God-given calling to, "Preach the word; be prepared in season and out of season; correct, rebuke and encourage—with great patience and careful instruction" (2 Timothy 4:2 NIV).

We preachers face the challenge daily: How to get and keep the attention of the listener to allow the Holy Spirit to accomplish His work in their mind. This is where rhetoric and logic and an engaging style of preaching come in. But it cannot end there. The primacy of Scripture is what the Holy Spirit works with and not our clever turn of phrase or captivating style. This is the message that Dr. Eves makes crystal clear in *Apologetics and Rhetoric*. Yes, there is a place for the well-crafted sermon that is based on a solid hermeneutic and sound exegesis of the text. But first and foremost, it is the primacy of Scripture and the efficacious work of the Holy Spirit that will open the ears of the nonbeliever and pierce through any intellectual or existential objections to truth that may be standing in their way of embracing the Way and the love of our Lord and Savior, Jesus Christ.

Apologetics and Rhetoric is a blueprint for ensuring that your sermon is relevant and thought-provoking in its scope and thoroughly Biblical and Spirit-blessed in its mission.

Rev. Rick Hiebert has been a pastor and National Church leader in the Pentecostal Assemblies of Canada for more than 40 years. From 1992 to 2004, he was Editor of Testimony, the official publication of the PAOC.

Synopsis

The purpose of this book is to challenge your method of preaching. This we know: God wants His Word proclaimed. Preaching is the proclamation of the Word of God and central and distinctive in the history of Christianity. Preaching, in its true sense, was never intended as a public expression of opinions but is centered on the redemptive work of Christ. God had chosen the "foolishness of preaching" as his instrument of salvation. Preaching was always central in the life of the early Church.

Only God's Word is able to convince, convert, and sanctify the soul. Thousands of years have gone by since these words were penned. Yet, the Word of God continues to be alive and active, transforming lives even today. God's Word produces spiritual results through the work of His Spirit. Preaching is God's primary method for making his will and his words known to the world. We need to do our part to make his words known.

This book will assist you in gaining an understanding of the subject of expository preaching to a postmodern world while incorporating rhetoric as well as apologetics. The challenging audience for today is postmodernists. When the Church thinks of postmodernism, we tend to believe these people are outside the Church, but in fact, postmodernists are also in the Church. Postmodernists are often challenging for the Church because many have questions that churches don't have answers for. The Church may find itself feeling awkward in light of postmodernists' skepticism, as the Church finds it difficult to reasonably answer or defend the Christian faith. Although many view postmodernists as argumentative or difficult, they are seeking certain truths. And often people need their tough questions answered at a time when the Church is not equipped to answer them.

Expository preaching should be an emphasis for those who are passionate about preaching to postmodernists. This holds true whether you are a seminary student or anyone else who desires a unique outlook on preaching. My goal is to impact how you preach and deliver the message of God biblically and passionately while defending the faith. The focus of this book is to build a bridge between the Word of the Lord and a postmodern world.

I researched the Biblical perspective and history of preaching. I use the past as a teacher for the present and future. Many attempt to reach the lost with new, modern methods and strategies, while leaving fundamental methods of Biblical preaching behind. I do not seek to do so. I have not attempted to reinvent preaching, but only to explain what the scriptures meant when Jesus began preaching and how the Lord encouraged his own to preach like him.

This method of preaching will not guarantee that a cynical, hostile postmodernist listener will agree with you. There are people in the world who argue just for the sake of arguing and have no interest in listening to you. But as long as your presentations are Spirit-driven, persuasive, and a reasoned rational defense, every message you deliver should be compelling.

You will discover that I have researched the history of expository preaching, apologetics, and rhetoric. My conclusions are not without support. There is a reason why I have encouraged expository preaching rather than other methods of preaching. I also give historical substantive reasons why I have included Rhetoric and Apologetics. By combining the Word of God with rhetoric and an explanation of the logic of the Word of God brings about a powerful combination that will move the postmodernist toward the Truth.

Rhetoric

Rhetoric (effective or persuasive speech) should be incorporated in preaching. The word "rhetoric" has been used in such a way that it has lost its original meaning. It now has a negative connotation. Many people consider rhetoric to be nothing more than a clever ploy. But I present an insightful history of rhetoric to show that it can be and was meant to be, used in an appropriate way. Rhetorical skills are very important in proclaiming the Gospel message, and there is more to it than just oratory skills.

Apologetics

Apologetics is a discipline that has often been overlooked within the context of preaching. But I believe Apologetics is a vital aspect of preaching. We never want to disregard the intellect and the intellectual. Many skeptics believe that Christianity is irrational and sadly Christians often cannot defend the faith rationally. According to the Bible:

"Always be ready to give a [logical] defense to anyone who asks you to account for the hope and confident assurance [elicited by faith] that is within you, yet [do it] with gentleness and respect" (2 Peter 3:15).

The objective of rational appeal is to affect the head and the heart. Apologetics can be used to eliminate or diminish the intellectual hurdles that hinder people from accepting God's word. False beliefs and ideas can be the single greatest obstacle to accepting the gospel message.

Preaching

When I began my research, I learned that people define the word "preaching" differently. I also realized that many preachers struggle to do it well. As a result, congregations often suffer in many ways. Their knowledge of God and His Word has never been developed. My concern is that so often people have spent years attending church but know very little about what matters most to God.

Preaching was designed to have an effect on the life of the listener. I am certain that many preachers in a figurative sense "throw their sermon at the wall and hope something sticks." I recognized that most people believe that when we are gathered in the church and someone is standing behind the pulpit speaking, that is considered preaching. Nothing could be further from the truth. Often sermons lack in substance and style, but even more, unfortunately, they lack in Scriptural content. Consequently, the congregation suffers.

I have attended a variety of Churches and have heard many sermons. They are, more often than not, just stories with very little Biblical content. Commonly, many use scripture as a springboard to deliver their message rather a foundation. It might be described as a story where the preacher applies the Word of God only sparingly enough to justify their message. The Word of God becomes an afterthought.

I personally believe in Expository Preaching. The aim of Expository Preaching is keeping the message in its true biblical context. The danger is that when the message is taken out of context, God is taken out of context. Expository Preaching has its foundation grounded in eternal truth. The truth of God's Word is liberating. Yet, the message should always speak to the listener's contemporary circumstances or it becomes nothing more than a history lesson. I sincerely believe that:

> "All scripture is given by inspiration of God, and is profitable for doctrine, for reproof, for correction, for instruction in righteousness" (2 Timothy 3:16).

There is no spiritual substitute for Scripture. The term "*inspiration,*" implies that God's supernatural Spirit abides within. Scripture is essential for sustaining spiritual life and for development in the Christian life. It is the Holy Spirit, the manifest power of God that operates through God's Word. Christ Himself declares in Matthew 4:4 and Deuteronomy 8:3:

> "Man shall not live on bread alone, but on every word that proceeds out of the mouth of God" (Deuteronomy 8:3).

As our physical being is nourished by nutritional food, our souls are nourished with the Word of God. Again, there is no substitute for God's Word.

In saying that this book is about delivery, I do not mean to suggest that you should ignore and neglect sound exegete of any sermon. I believe that sermons should be true to the Biblical text. All true Biblical sermons should be Christ-centered, or at the very least, Theo-Centric and theologically sound. I believe that a sermon can never be a sermon without sound hermeneutics (Biblical Interpretation). The fundamental hermeneutical standard is that every text must be understood in its context. In fact, you could never have a creditable sermon without solid hermeneutics.

Never let us forget the audience factor. Pulpit communication is vital and necessary for every sermon. Homiletics (*The Art of Preaching*) is often treated as a one-way communication that has disregarded the audience. We should do the very best we can to tailor the message to our audience.

Conclusion

There have been many brilliant books written on the subject of preaching. I have read many of them. I have also cited and listed in this book some suggested readings that are worthy of your time and study. It is my hope that this book will be insightful and contribute in the areas of which I have addressed. My many years as a student and adjunct professor at Trinity International University (South Florida Campus) helped me prepare for this task.

Introduction

In his book *Preaching with Purpose*, author Jay E. Adams says, "Men and women (and especially young people) are being turned away from Christ and His church by dull, unarresting, unedifying, and aimless preaching."[1] Many of these men and women are postmodernists. Traditionally, postmodernists have been viewed as a challenging audience to reach with the message of the Lord Jesus Christ. Graham Johnston reports in his book, *Preaching to a Postmodern World*, that "...two-thirds of Americans no longer believe in objective truth."[2] This number is not just restricted to the unchurched; it includes the churched, as well. Although postmodern beliefs can be cynical in nature, biblical preaching (empowered by God's Spirit) and God's Word (the good news) is full of certain hope.

Many churches either ignore the developing philosophy of postmodernism or respond to postmodernists in a negative way. To effectively reach the postmodern population, preaching must include both rhetoric and apologetics to speak gospel messages that are both potent and powerful enough to bring about life-changing outcomes. Implementing apologetics and rhetoric will bring about a reasonable, logical, and substantive defense for the Christian belief.

Christian apologetics involves the systematic use of information to present a rational argument for the Christian faith and to defend it against objections and misrepresentations. The English word *apologetics* comes from the Greek word *apologia*, which means, "to give a reason or defense, speaking in defense. As it concerns the Christian faith, then, apologetics has to do with defending, or making a case for, the truth of the Christian faith."[3]

Rhetoric is the arrangement of preaching the truth through the skill of eloquence, with a strong foundation of the knowledge of scripture. Grant R. Osborne put it this way in his book, *The Hermeneutical Spiral*: Rhetoric is "the art of discovering the best possible means of persuasion in regard to any subject whatever."[4] The intent is to persuasively convince an audience to accept an idea and logically strike down erroneous beliefs.

God wants everyone to hear and believe the gospel message. 2 Peter 3:9 declares, "It God's will that none shall perish." He has gone to great lengths to reach the lost. John 3:16 sums it up best by saying, "for God so loved the world that he sent his only begotten Son and whosoever believes in him shall not perish but will have everlasting life." By expanding the gospel message to the postmodern world through more effective preaching, which incorporates rhetoric and apologetics, Christian churches can reach both churched and unchurched postmodern audiences here in the United States with both reason and logic.

This book identifies the arguments, positions, and concerns of the Christian and the postmodern position and teaches Christians how to use the Bible to answer unbelieving postmodernists' objections to their faith. It should be noted that this book is written almost entirely from a research point of view and not from "experiences," though I have included a few. As such, it is chocked full of sources the reader can either purchase from a bookseller or check out of a library for further research if desired.

The concern from the Christian standpoint is that postmodernists believe all truth is subjective. It has become fashionable to accept that all beliefs are equal and that we live in a world of the unknown. In other words, the truth may be out there somewhere, but we will never capture it.

While postmodernists attempt to get along with our society as a whole, they are skeptical of a world filled with marketing ploys and every form of deception. I realize there are individuals who will not listen to any sound arguments and refuse to believe in the Lord Jesus Christ, but combining rhetoric and apologetics in preaching is the most effective way to persuade postmodernists of the truth.

Notes

1. Jay E. Adams, Preaching with Purpose (Grand Rapids MI: Zondervan, 1982), xi.
2. Graham Johnston, Preaching to a Postmodern World (Grand Rapids, MI: Baker Books, 2001), 8.
3. Steven B. Cowan, Five Views of Apologetics (Grand Rapids, MI: Zondervan Publishing House, 2000), 8.
4. Grant R. Osborne, The Hermeneutical Spiral (Downers Grove, IL: InterVarsity Press, 1991), 35.

CHAPTER 1
𝕽𝖍𝖊𝖙𝖔𝖗𝖎𝖈

According to James A. Herrick, author of *The History and Theory of Rhetoric*, Rhetoric is considered an art of discourse that comes from the "Greek: *techne* of *logos,* which means both 'word' and 'argument.'"[5] He says "Rhetorical discourse is usually intended to influence an audience to accept an idea, and then to act in a manner consistent with that idea."[6] Another definition comes from George Kennedy, who states in Herrick's book, "the energy inherent in emotion and thought, transmitted through the system of signs, including language, to others to influence their decisions or actions."[7] To have a deep understanding of what rhetoric is, we must look at its history. That way we will appreciate its meaning and develop a clearer understanding of why rhetoric is used as well as the importance of using it when preaching to the postmodern population.

Rhetoric had its beginnings in Italy, Greece, and Rome. In Greece, for example, there were no professional lawyers. In fact, O.C. Edwards, Jr., said in *A History of Preaching*, "Citizens had to argue their own cases in court, and some were better at it than others."[8] Individuals learned that a person who had rhetorical skills could persuade others to believe something their way. In fact, the Greek philosopher Aristotle held "that rhetoric's potential for advocating true ideas was one of the main reasons for studying the art."[9] Rhetoric, therefore, was soon perceived as a valuable tool and quickly adopted by people who wanted to influence the decisions of others.

Rhetoric became popular among affluent families who wanted to ensure leadership status and aristocratic success in court and legislative assemblies. Worldly success was viewed as being skilled and educated in eloquent speaking and in the art of verbal discourse. Eventually, rhetoric became the very basis of Greek education. The primary concern of rhetorical criticism is persuasion. No one wants to believe he or she has been manipulated or misled by unscrupulous people, or by anyone, for that matter.

A Brief History of Rhetoric

The exact beginning and history of rhetoric is rather difficult to pinpoint, but I will begin my historical study from the rise of classical rhetoric in ancient Greece, which lasted from the fifth through fourth centuries BC. Not that I suggest there was no rhetoric before the classical Greek world, but Greece considered rhetoric a high art, and as such developed it systemically to make it part of the cultural and national value. In fact, says Herrick, "...training in rhetoric became the foundation of Greek education and eventually came to be viewed as the principal sign of an educated and influential person."[10]

In about the fifth century B.C. citizens were tremendously handicapped at defending themselves in courts of law and found themselves at the mercy of the system, with little chance of success. A group of trained individuals called the Sophists came at a time when great skill in oratory was necessary. Herrick says, "Rhetoric as a systematic study, then, was developed by a group of orators, educators, and advocates called Sophists, a name derived from the Greek word *Sophos*, meaning wise or skilled."[11] The Sophists were greatly admired, though those who opposed them thought perhaps they were more concerned with rhetorical success than the truth. This was a time when the Greek society was changing from an aristocratic rule to a democratic society. Poulakos, a historian wrote (as quoted by Herrick), "When the Sophists appeared on the horizon of the Hellenic city states, they found themselves in the midst of an enormous cultural change: from aristocracy to democracy."[12]

An aristocracy (which means rule by the best) is a form of government in which a few elite, privileged, best-qualified citizens rule. Democracy, by contrast, is a form of government in which all adult citizens have an equal say in the decisions that affect their lives. As a result of the collapse of the aristocrats and the rise of a democratic society, the rights of freedom of speech and rhetoric became paramount in the Greek society.

According to Herrick, Sophists earned a reputation for "extravagant displays of language"[13] and for astonishing audiences with their "brilliant style...colorful appearances and flamboyant personalities."[14] Due to the skill of the Sophists, people would pay dearly to be trained to speak persuasively. Herrick says, "The Sophists' offered to teach rhetoric to anyone capable of paying their high fees must have appeared as a means of breaching the barriers separating these special classes and so affording entrance to previously inaccessible sources of power."[15] "With democratic reforms,"[16] continues Herrick, "the political life of the *polis* came to be managed by oratory and debate. It has been said that "tyrants may have ruled other nations by torture and the lash: the Greeks took their decisions by persuading and debate."[17]

According to a popular Sophist named Gorgias, who lived from (485 to 380 B.C.), a successful rhetorician could speak persuasively on a topic, irrespective of his experience in that field. Herrick says, "Gorgias was a teacher of rhetoric, a defender of the practice, and himself a professional persuader. He boasted of being able to persuade anyone of anything. His powers of persuasion were, indeed, legendary. For instance, he is reputed to have persuaded the Athenians to build a gold statue of him at Delphi, an honor unheard of for a foreigner, though some sources suggest he paid for the statue."[18] Nevertheless, Jaqueline de Romilly says in her book, *Magic and Rhetoric in Ancient Greece*, that "Gorgias believed that words worked their magic most powerfully arousing human emotions such as fear, pity, and longing."[19]

Aristotle actually stood as the most central figure of the classical Greek scholars of rhetoric because he provided the arrangement based on logic. Aristotle's discourse on rhetoric was an attempt to systematically define it as an art or skill, not limited to just political or civic recourse, but a communication method applicable to all fields. "Aristotle's approach to rhetoric was both pragmatic and scientific,"[20] says Herrick. "Rhetoric," he writes, "is the faculty (*dunamis:* also capacity, power) of observing in any given case available means of persuasion."[21] Aristotle believed there are three essential aspects to accomplishing the available means of persuasion: logos (rational appeal), pathos (emotional appeal), and ethos (ethical appeal). "These are intentionally used by rhetoricians to persuade an audience,"[22] says Edward Corbett, P.J. Corbet, and Robert J. Connors in their book *Classical Rhetoric for the Modern Student* (4th ed).

According to Aristotle, "Persuasion occurs through arguments [*logoi*] when we show the truth or the apparent truth from whatever is persuasive in each case."[23] The word logos refers to any effort to appeal to the intellect and would be considered the common meaning of a logical argument. Academic arguments rely on logos. Logical connections of reasoning are essential to support all arguments. Lucy Lind Hogan and Robert Reid write in their book, *Connecting with the Congregation,* that "Good rhetorical reasons, therefore, are reasons that are both truthful and compelling and convincing to the listener."[24] The Christian word *logos,* however, is not to be confused with the logos of the ancient philosophers. Aristotle used the word *logos* to refer to reasoned dialogue or argument in the field of rhetoric.

"The term *pathos,*" Herrick says, "is often used to refer to the affective or emotional appeals that give persuasive messages their power to move an audience to action, but Aristotle's interest in emotion has to do specifically with emotion's ability to affect the judgment of audiences."[25] This can be done through metaphor, amplification, storytelling, or presenting the topic in a way that evokes strong emotions in audience members and puts them in a certain frame of mind.

"According to Aristotle," continues Herrick, "*ethos* was potentially the most persuasive. When people are convinced that a speaker is knowledgeable, trustworthy, and has their best interests at heart, they will be very likely to accept as true what that speaker has to say."[26] Aristotle's view of *ethos* has been supported by many contemporary rhetorical scholars. More importantly, *ethos* or credibility is based on the personal character of the speaker, as the Greek word *arete* translates "moral excellence," which denotes someone with exceptional character or virtue.

The word *virtue* is considered a positive foundation of the principles of character and moral superiority. Hogan and Reid state that "Two issues, therefore, were of supreme importance; the character and the authority of the speaker. While these often appear as synonyms for *ethos*, it is crucial to see how these are different concepts that function quite differently."[27] This why Aristotle maintained that persuading others depends on making appeals based on who we are, on making appeals to their passion and aspirations, and on making appeals through arguments grounded in practical reasoning."[28]

Rome admired and valued the work of Greek rhetoricians such as Aristotle, so much so, that they incorporated and implemented rhetoric into their system. Marcus Tullius Cicero (106-43 B.C.) was considered one of Rome's greatest orators. Cicero revised Greek rhetoric to Roman purposes. Herrick observes that "the Romans adhered closely to Greek methods of rhetorical education."[29]

Cicero's first book on rhetoric linked wisdom and eloquence. Herrick quotes Cicero, who writes "I have been led by reason itself to hold this opinion first and foremost, that wisdom without eloquence does little for the good of states, but that eloquence without wisdom is generally highly disadvantageous and is never helpful."[30]

For the Romans, wisdom was paramount. According to James May, author of *Trials of Character: The Eloquence of Ciceronian Ethos,* wisdom to a Roman was "gained through practical experience, expert knowledge, and a sense of responsibility in both private and public life."[31] Cicero believed that the speaker should progress through the following five activities: choose the topic, arrange the speech in an orderly fashion, use style or figures of speech, memorize the foundations of the speech, and deliver the speech to the audience. Cicero believed that by proceeding through these steps "the orator can take a comprehensive view of the individual case in hand and duly take account of all its special circumstances. Only such an approach can produce a coherent speech that is as persuasive as the circumstances allow."[32]

According to Cicero, the three functions of the speaker are to teach, to delight, and to persuade … persuasion being the piece that moves the audience's emotions.[33] Quintilian, a Roman rhetorician, simplified the definition of an orator as "the good man speaking well."[34]

Later in church history, we read about St. Augustine of Hippo (A.D.350-430), who is known as one of the greatest early church fathers, and whom Herrick says "excelled at rhetoric and saw it as a path to wealth and fame."[35] Later in his life when he became a Christian, however, he understood the potential to abuse rhetoric. Thomas Aquinas, (1225-1274 AD), believed a preacher needs to instruct the intelligence, kindle the emotions, and form the will. "Preaching that did not intensify the emotions," he said, "would be as barren as preaching that did nothing for the minds or wills."[36]

The Puritans followed in the seventieth and eighteen centuries by gathering their doctrines from the Bible, utilizing logic to prove those doctrines, and employing the means of "rhetoric to make those doctrines attractive, reasons convincing, and applications efficacious."[37] Jonathan Edwards in the eighteenth century demonstrates this mode of preaching. His sermons invariably proceeded as follows: 1) text of Scripture 2) doctrine (presented logically from Scripture and theology) and 3) applications (using persuasive speech to appeal to the emotions of the listeners).

Unfortunately, during the Enlightenment period, rhetoric strayed from its original purpose and became more of a flowery speech having little or no significance other than to manipulate people. This ultimately influenced the current thinking about rhetoric.

In the twentieth century, however, Dr. Martin Luther King, Jr., realized the power of the spoken word … proving an appeal to the intellect, imagination, and the heart, according to Richard Lischer, author of *The Preacher King*.[38] Herrick also says that "Dr. King was a highly skillful and knowledgeable practitioner of the art of rhetoric. He, and others working with him, created a community of value and action. And much of their work was accomplished by means of effective rhetorical discourse."[39]

Contemporary biblical rhetorical criticism has returned to more of an Aristotelian mode that seeks to understand the persuasive power of dynamic biblical texts to move audiences to act on what he/she has heard. Bryan Chapell, in his book *Christ Centered Preaching*, makes an observation about 1 Thessalonians 1:5 in which the Apostle Paul writes under the inspiration the Holy Spirit: "Our gospel came unto you not simply with words [*logos*], but also with power, and with deep conviction [*pathos*]. You know how we live [*ethos*] among you for your sake."[40]

David-Dunn Wilson says in *A Mirror for the Church* that the epistles of Paul were written for proclamation: "The rhetorical elements which have been detected in the epistles support this view, since rhetoric was essentially the 'systematic study of oratory' designed to persuade those who read or hear. Bo Reicke argues that large parts of Paul's epistles are influenced by apostolic "oral discourses" designed as literary substitutes for personal addresses. Paul certainly sees his epistles as an extension of his personal preaching ministry, intended to be read publicly to congregations in order to correct their thinking."[41]

Why Rhetoric is Used in Preaching

The answer to this question lies in Augustine's, Cicero's, and Aristotle's contributions. In the days of the late Roman Empire (354-430), it was Augustine's influence that introduced it to Christian preaching. Rhetoric had already influenced his early education, so when he became a Christian he excelled in it and merged it with preaching. Augustine viewed rhetoric as a skill that preachers should use to preach the Truth, the Word of God, in a clear and stylistic manner. Herrick summarizes Cicero's view, which Augustine endorsed: "The preacher must know his subject matter in order to teach it well. He must know how to reach his congregation's emotions (to delight), and to persuade them to Christian living (to move)."[42] Augustine agreed with Cicero regarding that rhetoric should teach, delight, and persuade individuals, but only to move them to Christianity.

Augustine also said, as quoted in by Lischer: It is the duty, then, of the interpreter and teacher of the Holy Scripture, the defender of the true faith and the opponent of error, both to teach what is right and to refute what is wrong, and in the performance of this task to conciliate the hostile, to rouse the careless, and to tell the ignorant both what is occurring at present and what is probable in the future.[43]

Rhetoric then is required for effective preaching, which is based on a sound study of the scriptures. This is necessary in order to ensure sound doctrine and to teach the body of Christ through engaging members of the congregation and then motivating them to obey the Word of God.

Using Rhetoric When Preaching to Postmodernists

Effective use of rhetoric in preaching can be used to reach the postmodern population because according to *The Preachers Forum*, rhetoric "seeks to understand the actions people perform when they communicate to one another for the purposes of persuasion, the invitation to understand one another better and as a means to self-discovery or self-knowledge."[44] The Forum also points out that "knowledge of the operation of rhetoric also can help make us more sophisticated audience members for messages. By focusing less on lists of stylistic elements and more upon a classical understanding of persuasive rhetoric, rhetorical criticism takes us away from traditional readings of sacred texts and into the dimension of social interaction and transformation."[45]

The character of the preacher is also important. Rhetoric is not just about being an eloquent speaker; it is about one's moral character, connecting with the audience, and the delivery of the sermon. A postmodern audience is more likely to be persuaded by a credible source because it is more reliable. According to Hogan and Reid, "Good speakers shape how listeners view them as speakers (*ethos*), involve listeners emotionally (*pathos*), and shape the reasons offered by sifting through the possible arguments, making choices about what to include and what to exclude (*logos*). This is why Aristotle maintained that persuading others depends on making appeals based on who we are, on making appeals through arguments grounded in practical reasoning."[46]

Character does play a powerful role. I lived in the Northwest Territories of Canada for a number of years. As many times as I told the First Natives I was not a minister, they refused to believe it. My observation was that they determined whom I was based on my character. Alcohol in the Northwest Canadian territories, for example, is a large problem. I do not drink and therefore never went into the liquor store. Even if I had, I would have been viewed as another heavy drinker. Living in a small town, the word would have gotten out and hurt my credibility as an active member and volunteer at my church. The First Natives are not impressed with someone's title but the way someone lives out his or her life.

Character is also important in a court of law. Those in a courtroom are told to "Please rise, as the Honorable Judge [identified by name] enters the courtroom." After the judge seats himself or herself, the people in the courtroom are told to sit down. The position and title of the judge give the person instant authority. He or she is honored. The judge wears a distinguished robe and sits above all those in the courtroom. No one speaks unless he or she gives permission, and his or her judgment is final.

The bottom line is that rhetoric has had a long history of effectiveness. There is no denying that the oratory skills of powerful speakers of our time, such as Martin Luther King, Jr., continue to have a powerful effect on the lives of people today.

𝔑otes

5. James A. Herrick, *The History and Theory of Rhetoric* (New York, NY: Pearson, 2005), 36.
6. Ibid., 13.
7. Ibid., 5.
8. O.C. Edwards Jr., *A History of Preaching* (Nashville, TN: Abingdon Press, 2004), 12. Herrick, 19.
9. Herrick, 19.
10. Ibid., 35.
11. Ibid., 36.
12. Ibid., 56.
13. Ibid., 36.
14. Ibid.
15. Ibid., 34.
16. Ibid.
17. Ibid.
18. Ibid., 43.
19. Jacqueline de Romilly, Magic and Rhetoric in Ancient Greece (Cambridge, MA: Harvard University Press, 1975), 256.
20. Herrick, 78.
21. Ibid., 80.
22. Edward Corbett, P. J. Corbet & Robert J. Connors, Classical Rhetoric For the Modern Student (4th ed.) (New York, NY: Oxford University Press, 1999), 18.
23. Lucy Lind Hogan & Robert Reid, Connecting with the Congregation (Nashville, TN: Abingdon Press, 1999), 30.
24. Ibid., 94.
25. Herrick, 88.
26. Ibid., 90.
27. Hogan & Reid, 51.
28. Ibid., 95.
29. Herrick, 102.
30. Ibid.
31. James M. May, Trials of Character: The Eloquence of Ciceronian Ethos (Chapel Hill, NC: University of North Carolina Press, 1988), 6.
32. The Preachers Forum. "Exploring Rhetoric and Rhetorical Criticism," www. http://preachersforum.org/?page_id=80 (accessed 01-12-2014).

33. Herrick, 109.
34. Hogan & Reid, 30.
35. Herrick, 132.
36. George E. Sweazey, Preaching the Good News (Englewood, NJ: Prentice-Hall Inc., 1976), 22.
37. Perry Miller, The New England Mind, The Seventeenth Century (Cambridge, MA: Harvard University Press, 1983), 320-321.
38. Richard Lischer, The Preacher King (New York, NY: Oxford University Press, 1995), 38.
39. Herrick, 23.
40. Bryan Chapell, Christ-Centered Preaching (Grand Rapids, MI: Baker Academic, 1994), 35.
41. David-Dunn Wilson, A Mirror for the Church (Grand Rapids, MI: Eerdmans, 2005),13.
42. Herrick, 133.
43. Richard Lischer, Theories of Preaching: Selected Readings in the Homiletical Tradition (Durham, NC: The Labyrinth Press, 1987), 212.
44. The Preachers Forum, Exploring Rhetoric and Rhetorical Criticism, www. http://preachersforum.org/?page_id=80 (accessed 01-12-2014).
45. The Preachers Forum, parg. 8.
46. Hogan & Reid, 95

CHAPTER 2

Apologetics

The discipline of Christian apologetics is to utilize the systematic use of information, to present a rational argument for the Christian faith, and to defend the faith against objections and misrepresentation. The English word *apologetics* comes from the Greek word *apologia*, which means, "to give a reason or defense, speaking in defense."[47] Throughout history, the Christian church has been under attack for its beliefs and faith in God. Christianity has often been viewed as faith with no substance, but the church has responded by offering a defense for its faith. This meant applying Greek philosophy along with Christian scripture.

Apologetics is not just to be used defensively, however, but offensively as we are instructed to annihilate arguments against the Christian faith. 2 Corinthians 10:4-5 tells us, "For the weapons of our warfare are not carnal, but mighty through God to the pulling down of strong holds; Casting down imaginations, and every high thing that exalteth itself against the knowledge of God, and bringing into captivity every thought to the obedience of Christ." John M. Frame says in his book *The Doctrine of Knowledge of God* that "Believers are to stand for God's wisdom against false teaching, even under the most difficult challenges."[48]

𝔚𝔥𝔶 𝔄𝔭𝔬𝔩𝔬𝔤𝔢𝔱𝔦𝔠𝔰?

The answer to this question is because we are rational creatures and therefore, "must be approached with reasons."[49] Reasoning is not evil. God created humanity with reason, and we all attempt to make rational explanations. Each of us puts our socks on before our shoes. We bundle up when we are about to go out into the cold. We fill our gas tanks before going on a trip. Some Christians believe, however, that we do not need apologetics to win others to the faith. This seems almost ridiculous given that we rationalize everything in life, so why not Christianity?

"If reason were silenced, complains the philosopher, believers would have no way of answering an idolater who held up a piece of wood and demanded that it be adored as God! At the very least, says the philosopher, reason is needed to select what authority one is going to follow."[50] Dulles also says that "Those who reject reason almost inevitably fall into one of two traps. Some find themselves sucked into superstition, giving credence to what is demonstrably false. Others sink into unbelief or skepticism, rejecting what could be authenticated as worthy of belief."[51]

We can actually reason the resurrection of the Lord Jesus Christ by reading what He and others who witnessed it said about it. 1 Corinthians 15:4-8 says, for example: "And that he was buried, and that rose again the third day according to the scripture; And that he was seen of Cephas, then the twelve: After that, he was seen of above five hundred brethren at once; of whom the greater part remain unto this present, but some have fallen asleep. After that, he was seen of James; then of all the apostles. And last of all he was seen of me also, as of one born out of due time."

So, a large number of witnesses including the five hundred, Cephas, James, and Paul witnessed Christ's resurrection and were reached with that truth through reason. Luke also wrote in Acts 1:3, "To these He also presented Himself alive after His suffering, by many convincing proofs, appearing to them *over a period of* forty days and speaking of the things concerning the kingdom of God."

Before becoming a Christian, I was a private investigator for eight years. In my world, it was unimaginable to draw any conclusions without first having evidence to support a claim. We can speculate all we want on any given case, but without substantial evidence, we have nothing, only an interesting story at best. The strongest cases are those with strong evidence. Everything else is a mere assumption.

Having said that, based on this evidence, if we were in any court of law for criminal proceedings and had as many eyewitnesses interrogated (more than five hundred), the case would come to a quick conclusion because eye witness accounts are invaluable to establish any case. Even the Bible supports at least two or three witnesses to establish a case: Numbers 35:30; Deuteronomy 17:6; Matthew 18:16; John 8:17; 2 Corinthians 13:1; 1 Timothy 5:19.

The number of witnesses to Christ's resurrection far exceeds what is necessary to establish a case. We might refer to this as extraordinary evidence. According to Norman L. Geisler and Frank Turek in *I Don't have Enough Faith to be an Atheist*, "If 'extraordinary' means more than usual, then that's exactly what we have to do to support the Resurrection. We have more eyewitness's documents and earlier eyewitness's documents for the resurrection than for anything else in the ancient world."[52] The resurrection account was not based on some useless assertion; the Apostles proclaimed, as Luke recorded the account in Acts 1:3, "Since I myself have carefully investigated everything from the beginning, it seemed good also to me to write an orderly account for you, most excellent Theophilus."

Luke's objective was to write with the utmost accuracy and care. He writes in Acts 2:32 that "God has raised this Jesus to life, and we are all witnesses of the fact" and in Acts 3:15, "You killed the author of life, but God raised him from the dead. We are witnesses of this of this." John wrote in 1 John 1:1, "That which was from the beginning, which we have heard, which we have seen with our eyes, which we have looked at and our hands have touched – this we proclaim concerning the Word of life." Concerning the Apostle Paul's reference to 1 Corinthians 15, William Lillie, makes an interesting point in

Geisler and Turek's writings: "What gives a special authority to the list as historical evidence is the reference to most of the five hundred brethren being still alive. St. Paul says in effect: "if you do not believe me, you ask them." Such a statement in an admittedly genuine letter written within thirty years of the event is almost as strong evidence as one could hope to get for something that happened nearly two thousand years ago."[53]

How Apologetics Began in Christianity

In the first century, the Bible was simply presented as a proclamation of truth: Christ was born of a virgin and conceived by the Holy Spirit; He was crucified, buried, and raised from the dead on the third day; and He is now seated at the right hand of God the Father, as foretold by the Scriptures and recorded in 1 Corinthians 15:4 and Luke 24:46. That's because Christians at this time were concerned with establishing the faith with the proclamation of the Gospel. Avery Cardinal Dulles said in *A History of Apologetics*, "It began as a conviction that Jesus was Messiah and Lord, and this conviction seems to have drawn its overpowering force from the event of the Resurrection. As the message concerning Jesus as risen Lord was proclaimed, it gave rise to certain questions and objections from inquirers, from believers, and adversaries."[54]

This was during a time when the Roman Empire was the major world power and the Roman Emperor legally determined theological truth. Dunn-Wilson says, "… the Romans were eager to invoke the support of many gods. The Romans believed that by absorbing foreign cults into the state system, and they seem willing to include the Christianity and their God in this process."[55] Dunn-Wilson adds that Roman Emperor Severus Alexander (222-35), "respect[ed] the privilege of the Jews and allows Christians to exist unmolested, erecting statues to holy souls, including Christ, Abraham, Orpheus, and others."[56] For some Christians, this seemed a healthy compromise. For many others, however, it was abhorrent as they rejected any form of syncretism.

Initially, Rome believed Christianity was just an offshoot of Judaism, particularly since the Jewish people primarily lived privately. Christians, on the other hand, openly and actively proselytized with the intent of reaching the entire world with their beliefs. They worshipped God, refused to worship the emperor, and convinced others to do the same. Marvin Perry et al. said in his book *Western Civilization*: "As the number of Christians increased, Roman officials began to fear the Christians as subversives, preaching allegiance to God and not to Rome, and as a self-absorbed sect that did not want to fit into the Empire. To many Romans, Christians were disloyal citizens, strange people who would not accept the state gods, would not engage in sacrifices to Roman divinities, scorned gladiatorial contests, stayed away from public baths, glorified none violence, refused to honor deceased emperors as gods, and worshipped a crucified criminal as Lord."[57]

At that point, the Roman authorities, as well as the general population, realized that Christians were fundamentally different. They lived a life of holiness quite contrary to the pagan way of life. Bruce L. Shelley says in his book, *Church History in Plain Language,* that "Other social events Christians rejected because they found them wrong in themselves. Gladiator combats, for example, were to the Christian inhuman. In amphitheaters all across the empire, the Romans forced prisoners of war and slaves to fight with each to the death, just for the amusement of the crowd."[58] So the Roman Empire and Christians were clearly on a collision course because Christianity contradicted common Roman beliefs. Christianity also created an air of suspicion and frightened the public, largely because Christians often held private or secret meetings and did not involve themselves with the general population.

By the first quarter of the second century, slanderous accusations from the government were leveled against the Christian community for refusing to worship the emperor of Rome and the gods of the state. They were also said to be involved with cannibalism because of the practice of the Lord's Supper. And finally, largely due to the secrecy of their meetings, the Christian community was accused of gross immorality and attracting the uneducated and low-income individuals.

As a result of all these accusations, apologetics became necessary for Christians to defend their faith against rumors and false allegations from the pagan community as well as persecution from the state. Dunn-Wilson contends: "However, despite all opposition, the congregations are swelled by increasing numbers of educated and influential converts. This gives the lie to Celsius (a 2nd-century Greek philosopher and a critic of Early Christianity) that Christianity attracts only 'youngsters and mobs of domestics' and confirms Origen's boast that 'an abundance of intelligent hearers' now joins congregations, thirsting for 'noble doctrines of the faith.' It becomes clear that the church needs preachers who can meet their congregations' intellectual demands, alert them to spiritual dangers that threaten them, and convince them of Christianity's eventual triumph."[59]

Apologetics, therefore, became the most characteristic form of Christian writing at the beginning of the second century. This was when Christian writers became known as apologists. Of the many apologists from this time, the most noteworthy was Justin Martyr (ca. 100-165), who according to Dulles, was primarily concerned with "winning civil toleration for Christians."[60] So in his two *Apologies*, according to Kenneth Boa and Robert M. Bowman, authors of *Faith has its Reasons Integrative Approach Defending Christian Faith*, "he ... argued that it was in fact the true philosophy..... he refuted common errors and rumors (for example, that Christians were atheists and that they ate flesh and drank blood) and presented Christianity as a morally superior religion."[61]

Not everyone in the church agreed with apologetics as a means of defending the faith, however. Church father Tertullian (c.160–230 CE), believed that apologetics represented Greece and faith represented Jerusalem, hence his famous quote, "What indeed has Athens to do with Jerusalem?" The church should therefore not combine the church's beliefs with the pagan Greco-Roman philosophies. Tertullian said (as quoted in Marvin Perry et al.'s *Western Civilization: Ideas, Politics, And Society*), "With our faith, we desire no further belief. For this is our faith that there is nothing which we ought to believe besides."[62]

Tertullian rejected worldly knowledge and wisdom, claiming not all can be sufficiently known through logic and reason. It was not necessary therefore to defend the faith because faith in God is sufficient for all our needs. Tertullian and others who hold this view are tagged as fideists, who believed Christians should have complete reliance on God and his Word. This belief remains a center of contention among contemporary philosophers of religion. "The Spirit's work is not to persuade us of something for which there is no rational grounds, but rather to persuade us by illuminating the rational grounds which obligate us to believe. Spirit-created faith is not blind."[63]

Others, however, did not reject Greek education and philosophy, and embraced both faith and reason: Perry et al. say, "Knowledge of Greek philosophy, they contended, helped Christians explain their beliefs logically and argue intellectually with pagan critics of Christian teachings."[64] Today, scholars such as R.C. Sproul, Arthur Lindsley, & John Gerstner, in their book, *Classical Apologetics*, maintain, "Apologetics is the reasoned defense of the Christian religion. Christianity is a faith, to be sure; but there are reasons for the faith. Faith is not to be confused with reason; but neither is it to be separated from it."[65]

Even today Christians as a whole believe that God's Spirit indwells us. Some Christians will even say the Spirit of God will just "give it to us." In other words, he will teach us and guide us in what we should say, so there is no need for a Greek or Roman influence to infiltrate the church and God's people. Matthew 10:17-20 is one of the primary scriptures used against apologetics: "But when they hand you over, do not worry about how or what you are to say; for it will be given you in that hour what you are to say. For it is not you who speak, but it is the Spirit of your Father who speaks in you." This passage is about anxiety and fear. Biblically, no matter what the situation in life, God never abandons his people.

The Apostles were clearly guided by the Lord. God alone divinely inspired the Apostle Paul to write almost half of the twenty-seven New Testament books. Acts 4:13 describes the Apostles as "unlearned and ignorant men," but who "had been with Jesus." No one except Paul had been rabbinically schooled; they were educated by Christ himself for three-and-a-half years. Most also believe Moses penned the first five books of the Bible. Acts 7:22 tells us that "Moses was learned in all the wisdom of the Egyptians, and was mighty in words and in deeds."

So, of course, the Gospel cannot be properly proclaimed without the Lord's guidance, which today manifests in the presence of the Holy Spirit indwelt in all believers. In fact 2 Timothy 3:1 says the inspired Word of God contains the Spirit of God: "For all scripture is given by inspiration of God," and 2 Timothy 2:15 is clear that we are to "Study to show thyself approved unto God, a workman that need not to be ashamed, rightly dividing the word of truth." So, the Spirit of God is no replacement for study and preparation. William Barclay says in his book, *The Promise of the Spirit*, "It is not that the Holy Spirit was a substitute for careful thought; it was not that the Holy Spirit absolved a man from the duty of thinking and planning."[66]

Having said that, as effective as apologetics are, they are not a substitute for the Holy Spirit. However, they can be used effectively as the Spirit helps us as we do our part when preaching the Gospel to all nations.

Biblical Support for Apologetics

The Bible supports the use of apologetics. In Acts 17, the Apostle Paul offered an apologetic defense in Athens on Mars Hill, known as one of the world's greatest learning center. Idols, an invention of humanity's imagination built with human hands, surrounded him. The Apostle Paul may have been shocked by the Athenians' lack of religious knowledge, even though they were known for their great learning. Their ignorance of the one true God, however, simply demonstrated how foolish they were. The Athenians were known for their superior wisdom, but within the city stood a statue that read "to an unknown God." So even though the Greeks prided themselves on their knowledge, they admittedly knew nothing of this God. The Apostle Paul, however, was able to make a strong defense by preaching the Gospel while applying apologetics and directing their attention to the natural world in which we all live.

Paul also made use of the specific phrase "defending the gospel" in Philippians 1:7, 16 and said, "I make my defense" in Acts 26:2 during his trial before Festus and Agrippa. He did not care who was in his audience. He simply used his Damascus road experience to proclaim how Christ revealed himself to him and completely transformed his life. 1 Peter 3:15 states, "But sanctify the Lord God in your hearts: and be ready always to give an answer to every man that asks you a reason of the hope that is in you with meekness and fear." So we can see from the Word of God that Christian apologetics has two goals, says Craig Loscalzo in his book, *Apologetic Preaching*: "1) to present unbelievers with a viable understanding of the Christian faith so they may want to make it theirs, and 2) to instruct, confirm, and affirm those who are already believers in the faith."[67]

Interestingly enough, New Testament writers did not normally engage in arguments with unbelievers or tell them why they should be Christians. Instead, they simply proclaimed the message of Christ. This approach gave rise to questions being asked from the believers as well as unbelievers as they pertained to faith in Christ. According to Steven B. Cowan and Stanley N. Gundry in their book, *Five Views of Apologetics*, "Since the Enlightenment there has been a demand to expose all of our beliefs to the searching criticism of reason. If a belief is unsupported by evidence, it is irrational to believe it."[68] So we as believers should not argue just to argue but instead do what 2 Timothy 2:23 says: "refuse foolish and ignorant speculations, knowing they produce quarrels."

𝕬𝖕𝖔𝖑𝖔𝖌𝖊𝖙𝖎𝖈 𝕸𝖊𝖙𝖍𝖔𝖉𝖘

𝕬𝖗𝖌𝖚𝖒𝖊𝖓𝖙 𝖋𝖗𝖔𝖒 𝕲𝖊𝖓𝖊𝖗𝖆𝖑 𝕽𝖊𝖛𝖊𝖑𝖆𝖙𝖎𝖔𝖓

God in his wisdom has given humanity an opportunity by way of his creation, for the believer and the postmodernists to find neutral ground. "The knowledge of God's existence, character, and moral law, which comes through creation to all humanity is called "general revelation" (because it comes to all people generally),[69] says Henry Clarence Thiessen, in his book, *Introductory Lectures in Systematic Theology.*

I do not suggest this type of revelation can lead people to salvation, but rather as Romans 1:19-20 says, "… what can be known about God is plain to them, because God has shown it to them. Ever since the creation of the world his invisible nature, namely, his eternal power and deity, has been clearly perceived in the things that have been made. So they are without excuse." The only biblical reason for not plainly seeing God in the creation is to suppress the truth even though the truth is plainly seen. In general revelation, R.C. Sproul et al. say in *Classical Apologetics,* that "God is not immediately known but is known via a standard which points beyond itself to God, which is the world of nature. We are confronted by God's revelation in nature. By viewing nature, the mind is able to know the God of nature."[70]

While I'm not suggesting postmodernists, or anyone else, will be saved by looking at creation, I am suggesting that Christians and postmodernists can find common ground on numerous matters here. For understanding, God's creation does not require special revelation or knowledge. Nature itself points to God, and it would be reasonable to have a basic knowledge of God through the creation of things. To reject God after seeing his creation would mean rejecting what we can plainly see and know to be true.

When it comes to salvation, however, the Apostle Paul affirms a universal standard: that salvation is granted to all who call on the name of the Lord as Romans 10:13 reads: "How then will they call on Him in whom they have not believed? How will they believe in Him whom they have not heard? And how will they hear without a preacher?"

Argument from Design (the Teleological Argument)

The basis of the design argument is the evidence of order that there is a purpose and a design or a direction in nature. British philosopher William Paley is best known for the design theory. His approach was not only convincing but was presented in such a way that the people reading it could relate to as well as understand his analogies. According to L. Russ Bush, author of *Classical Readings in Christian Apologetics*, Paley "had a gift of effectively stating plain arguments in a way that made them very convincing to people even though he gathered his information from ordinary sources of reference."[71]

A proponent of the teleological argument, such as Paley, would say (as quoted in Stephen T. Davis' *God, Reason, and Theistic Proofs*, "How could the world have turned out with this sort of intricate harmony and sublime beauty unless it were designed by God."[72] He was not the originator of this theory, however, though he made it famous by stating (again, as quoted in Davis), "Where there is a telescope there must be a telescope maker."[73]

In 1802, Paley wrote a book called *Natural Theology*, applying the analogy of a watch's design to the idea that creation is designed, and therefore must have a designer. At the time Paley wrote the book, the British were the predominant clockmakers of the 17th and 18th centuries, and the watch was a relatively new invention. People were fascinated not only by its beauty and function (to keep time) but also by its complex mechanics. He said as quoted in Davis, "Its several parts are framed and put together for a purpose, viz. the purpose of telling time."[74] So Paley was able to show that like the watch, the universe with all its beauty and complexity also has an intelligent designer behind the design.

According to Geisler and Turek, "Scientists are now finding that the universe in which we live is like that diamond-studded Rolex, except the universe is even more precisely designed than the watch. In fact, the universe is specifically tweaked to enable life on earth--planet with scores of improbable and interdependent life-supporting conditions that make it a tiny oasis in a vast and hostile universe."[75]

Others throughout history have discussed the basic elements of the design theory. Perhaps the earliest philosophically rigorous version of the design argument owes to Thomas Aquinas (A.D. 1225-74), who was a proponent of natural theology. He suggested "Five Ways" to argue for the existence of God. He wrote: "We see that things, which lack knowledge, such as natural bodies, act for an end, and this is evident from their acting always, or nearly always, in the same way, so as to obtain the best result. Hence, it is plain that they achieve their end, not fortuitously, but designedly. Now whatever lacks knowledge cannot move towards an end, unless it be directed by some being endowed with knowledge and intelligence; as the arrow is directed by the archer. Therefore some intelligent being exists by whom all natural things are directed to their end; and this being we call God."[76]

Other writings of the design theory can be seen as far back as 200 A.D. when a philosopher named Galen of Pergamon wrote, as quoted in Paul A. Zimmerman's book, *Darwin, Evolution, and Creation*: "How can a man of any intelligence refer all this to chance as its cause; or if he denies this to be the effect of foresight and skill, I would ask what is there that foresight and skill do effect? For surely where chance or accident act, we do not see this correspondence and regularity of parts. Was it chance that made the skin give way to produce a mouth? Or, if this happened by chance also place teeth and a tongue within the mouth? For, if so, why should there not be teeth and a tongue in the nostrils or in the ear?"[77]

Finally, Aristotle (c. 469-399 B.C.) believed in the design theory and argued that the adaptation of human parts to one another, such as the eyelids protecting the eyeballs, could not have been due to chance and was a sign of a wise designer planning in the universe.

Present-Day Apologetic Preaching and the Postmodernist

Today, postmodernists often attack the Bible, despising it as God's authoritative Word. They often say the Bible contains countless errors. Either through misinformation or ignorance, many postmodernists believe the Bible doesn't have any true value. Often, however, these postmodernists have never read the Bible; they've just heard opinions on a subject they know little about and have subsequently formed opinions based on sound bites and speculative knowledge. As a result, many believe the Bible is irrelevant to contemporary society.

Unfortunately, we as believers haven't provided solid answers to their questions and skepticism. Instead, we have quoted 2 Corinthians 5:7 at them, "we are to walk by faith and not by sight," and defended our faith with such statements as "the Bible says so." It's always been my observation that most Christians have no comprehensive footing for their faith. Their weak defenses may be satisfactory for some believers but not satisfactory for all and certainly not for postmodernists, humanists, atheists, agnostics, cults, or any other group that comes against the Christian faith.

Although we as believers view the Bible as our foundation to ensure sound theology, we must reach the listener not with compromise or criticism, but begin where they are. When confronting postmodernists, our first instinct is usually to criticize their skepticism and their thinking, or retreat and avoid them. But even though Thomas, one of Christ's own disciples, would not believe, "except I shall see in his hands the print of the nails, and put my finger into the print of the nails, and thrust my hand into his side" (John 20:25), Jesus didn't find Thomas' request unreasonable or show any apprehension in answering his question. He simply told him in John 20:27, "reach here your finger, and see my hands; and reach here your hand, and put it into my side; and be not unbelieving, but believing." So rather than condemning Thomas, Christ simply showed him why he should believe by leading him to himself. We need to follow that example and not condemn but lead the postmodernists to the Lord.

Loscalzo agrees that postmodernists are exceedingly skeptical about everything and everybody, including God and the church. He believes these listeners would not accept the gospel as it has been presented in times past, that is, we are sinners in need of a Savior, but they might understand and accept it if they heard it from the apologetic perspective.

Loscalzo claims that postmodernists are living between the times, as life in the days of the Apostles were quite different from today. The author describes postmodernists as reasoning subjectively rather than objectively. They hunger after stories, which explains why many in our society gravitate to Doctor Phil and Oprah Winfrey-type programs. To postmodernists, there is no absolute truth, but many truths and every opinion and belief is as worthy as all others. So he/she has difficulty accepting biblical truth.

Postmodernists still live in the mindset of the famous 1960s self-help bestseller *I'm OK-You're OK*. They will shop for a church that aligns with their beliefs and their level of comfort. Loscalzo states, "If the cross of Christianity is too gruesome, they can choose the pacifism of the Buddha."[78] They also have a need for political correctness and community. So, a postmodernist would never accept a statement that he or she is a sinner. Loscalzo claims, therefore, that sermons should be presented inductively, as many Bible stories are offered, rather than deductively. This he believes is more suitable to the postmodernist societies that prefer stories.

Johnston, says of the postmodern generation, however, that "... the tough appearance only serves to hide their deep-seated fear, but beneath the exterior lurks a yearning for something profound, meaningful, and beautiful. Biblical preaching must hold out the word of life (Phil. 2:16)."[79] The question, he says, though, is what are the results of the method? Lischer says in his book, *A Theology of Preaching*, "What has passed for theology does not draw its life from the Gospel and is therefore utterly incapable of transforming lives or teaching or leading the church."[80]

The gospel, on the other hand, has a history of transforming and changing the lives of individuals. This is why postmodernists need to hear sound truth, backed up with solid explanations to satisfy their skepticism and questions so they will not "heap to themselves teachers after their own lusts," as 2 Timothy 4:3 says. There's no more pleasant sound to someone's "itching ears" than God's transformative power.

Notes

47. Stanley N. Gundry & Steven B. Cowan, Five Views on Apologetics (Grand Rapids, MI: Zondervan, 2000), 8.

48. John M. Frame. The Doctrine of the Knowledge of God (Phillipsburg, NJ: P & R Publishing, 1987), 124.

49. R. C. Sproul et al. Classical Apologetics (Grand Rapids, MI: Zondervan Publishing House, 1984), 16.

50. Avery Cardinal Dulles. A History of Apologetics (San Francisco, CA: Modern Apologetics Library, 1999), 108.

51. Dulles, xxv.

52. Norman L. Geisler & Frank Turek, I Don't Have Enough Faith to be an Atheist (Wheaton, IL: Crossway Books, 2004), 321.

53. Ibid., 243.

54. Dulles. A History of Apologetics, 1.

55. Dunn-Wilson, 34.

56. Ibid., 34.

57. Marvin Perry et al. Western Civilization (New York, NY: Houghton Mifflin Harcourt Company, 2009), 181.

58. Bruce L. Shelley, Church History in Plain Language (Dallas TX: Word Publishing, 1995), 39.

59. Dunn-Wilson, 35.

60. Dulles, 31.

61. Kenneth Boa, Robert M. Bowman. Faith has its Reasons: Integrative Approach to Defending the Christian Faith (Downers Grove, IL: InterVarsity Press, 2005), 14.

62. Marvin Perry et al., Western Civilization: Ideas, Politics, and Society (Boston, MA: Houghton Mifflin Harcourt Publishing Company, 2009), 182.

63. John M. Frame, Apologetics to the Glory of God (Phillipsburg, NJ: P & R Publishing, 1994), 136.

64. Perry et al., 183.

65. R.C. Sproul, Arthur Lindsley, & John Gerstner, Classical Apologetics (Grand Rapids, MI: Zondervan Publishing House, 1984), 13.

66. William Barclay. The Promise of the Spirit (Philadelphia, PA: The Westminster Press, 1960), 57.

67. Craig Loscalzo. Apologetic Preaching: Proclaiming Christ to a Postmodern World (InterVarsity Press, Downers Grove, IL, 2000), 25.

68. Steven B. Cowan and Stanley N. Gundry. Five Views of Apologetics (Grand Rapids, MI: Zondervan, 2000), 67.

69. Henry Clarence Thiessen. Introductory Lectures in Systematic Theology (Grand Rapids, MI: WM. B. Eerdmans Publishing Company, 1949), 122.

70. Classical Apologetics, 44.

71. L. Russ Bush. Classical Readings in Christian Apologetics (Grand Rapids, MI: Academia Books, 1983), 350.

72. Stephen T. Davis, God, Reason and Theistic Proofs (Grand Rapids, MI: WM B. Eerdmans Publishing Company, 1997), 97.

73. Davis, 99.

74. Ibid.

75. Geisler & Turek, 96.

76. Thomas Aquinas. Aquinas Summa Theological (Notre Dame, IN: Ave Maria Press., 1989), 2.

77. Paul A. Zimmerman. Darwin, Evolution, and Creation (Saint Louis, MO: Concordia Publishing House, 1959), 84.

78. Apologetic Preaching, 13.

79. Johnston, 140.

80. Richard Lischer, A Theology of Preaching (Eugene, OR: Wipf and Stock Publishers, 1992), 4.

CHAPTER 3

The Emergence of Postmodernism

Postmodernism had its beginnings in Modernism, known as the days of Enlightenment, roughly from the early 1700s to the 1950s. Whereas religion had once held and dominated the world as the source of absolute truth, in the days of Enlightenment (modernism) God and religion had taken a back seat to secular humanism, which modernists held supreme. As a result, secular humanists no longer felt restrained by religion and instead encouraged philosophical thinking to grow and develop in every area of life. According to Johnston, "The church found itself in mortal combat with the forces of secular humanism, which had abandoned God and the need for faith."[81]

As modernism was optimistic about life and the future, Johnston says, "In the postmodern world people are no longer convinced that knowledge is inherently good. In eschewing the Enlightenment myth of inevitable progress, postmodernism replaces the optimism of the last century with a gnawing pessimism..."[82]

Whereas modernists believed they were a progressive force that solved social ills through technology, postmodernists believe humanism has failed miserably in its attempt. Steven D. Mathewson, author of *The Art of Preaching Old Testament Narrative*, observes, "German philosopher Friedrich Nietzsche introduced a postmodern perspective when he suggested that what we think we know we really do not know."[83]

Where modernism manifested human self-confidence and self-congratulation, post-modernism is a confession of modesty, if not despair. For the postmodernist, there is no truth, only truths with lots of options. "Postmodernism and popular relativism," according to Graeme Goldworthy, author of *Preaching the Whole Bible as Christian Scripture*, are "expressions of ideological atheism that must be resisted."[84] As Kevin J. Vanhoozer observes in *Is There a Meaning in This Text?* "Postmodernism is a challenge to the Gospel because it grows out of the philosophy of the death of God."[85]

Attempting to remove God from life only results in spiritual barrenness and emotional distress. As a result, confusion reigns. "Without external standards (truth and morality) and without internal standards (a sense of self and dignity), there is only cynicism, panic, and free fall," contends Johnston.[86] "There are no principles, only preferences. There is no grand reason, only a reason,"[87] says John J. Stott in his book, *Evangelical Truth: A Personal Plea for Unity, Integrity, & Faithfulness*. "If post-modernism is correct, we cannot even aspire after truth, objectivity, universality and reality."[88]

Whereas modernists were relatively optimistic about life and the world in which they lived, the postmodernists are pessimistic about nearly everything. Chesterton warned (as quoted by Johnston)," when people cease believing in God, it's not that they believe in nothing, but they'll believe in anything."[89]

Postmodernist Thoughts on the Gospel

As a result of their cynicism, postmodernists often question every form of authority such as government and religion. So even though the Bible declares itself to be the Word of God according to 2 Timothy 3:16, postmodernists tend to regard the Bible as any other book. The challenge for the minister, however, is still to build a bridge between the secular world and the scriptures, so that people not only to hear but believe what the scriptures say. Unfortunately, "For postmoderns, discussing the Word is always to be preferred over obeying it," says Mathewson.[90] Even still, Vanhoozer observes that "...too many 'postmodernists' fail to notice the philosophical beam in their own eye, failing consistently to practice what they preach: they seek justice for 'others,' but they refuse to give 'authors' their due."[91]

The fact is, postmodernists are just like everyone else in this world, in need of a Savior. Scott M. Gibson makes this point in his book, *Preaching to a Shifting Culture*: "The Word has power to convict (Hebrews 4:12), to covert (1 Peter 1:23), and to transform (John 17:17) people of all times and places, and our job is to simply herald it."[92] The problem when preaching to postmodernists is that they struggle when pointed to the only source of truth. From their perspective, right and wrong is only a matter of perspective because there are no absolutes. Truth is a small "t" and is reduced to an illusion.

From the biblical perspective, however, the Word is Truth. It is unique in that it was written by men, yet inspired by God. While this belief could be an obstacle for the postmodernists, the scriptures are clear that our God is "the living God."

Postmodernists need to be approached from solid positions because of their "truth is relative" beliefs. They need to hear messages that contend, for example, that Christ is not only a biblical person, but that his life can be substantiated in history. Sermons should be well thought out with structure as well as clarity.

As far as venues, postmodernists prefer a non-threatening coffeehouse, where conversations take place more freely, and friendships develop, rather than a church building. They feel this is the best way to share life experiences, testimonies, and meaningful dialogue to develop relationships over time, which means those who seek to reach postmodernists will need to hold coffeehouse-type meetings repetitively and over a period of time.

While we should not fall into the trap of giving too much credence to the thoughts and minds of the postmodernists, it is still imperative that we reach them with the gospel message, which means we must first understand that audience. In the process, however, let us not forget that Hebrews 4:12 declares "the Word of God is quick and powerful and sharper than any two-edged sword." It has a history of rising up to bring down kingdoms and transform lives.

The Word of God has not lost its power. We should, therefore, continue to elevate the name of Jesus and, at the same time, always be aware of the diversity of our audience. Christians should adjust the message to the listener, the same way Paul did when he spoke differently in Acts 17 to the men of Athens at Mars Hill than he did to the Jews. When addressing the Jews, Paul confronted them with the scriptures. To the Greeks, he confronted them with natural theology. He did not relax the truth; he simply understood who his listeners were so he could always do as 1 Peter 3:15 instructs, "But sanctify the Lord God in your hearts: and be ready always to give an answer to every man that asketh you a reason of the hope that is in you with meakness and fear," and at the same time give an answer that his audience would understand and grasp.

Notes

81. Johnston, 25.
82. Ibid., 26.
83. Steven D. Mathewson, The Art of Preaching Old Testament Narrative (Ada, MI: Baker Academic, 2002), 35.
84. Graeme Goldworthy, Preaching the Whole Bible as Christian Scripture (Grand Rapids, MI: William B. Eerdmans Publishing Company, 2000), 13.
85. Kevin J. Vanhoozer, Is There a Meaning in This Text? (Grand Rapids, MI: Zondervan, 1998), 3.
86. Johnston, 39.
87. John J. Stott, Evangelical Truth: A Personal Plea for Unity, Integrity, & Faithfulness (Downers Grove, IL: InterVarsity Press, 1999), 45.
88. Ibid.
89. Johnston, 43.
90. Mathewson, 47.
91. Vanhoozer, 3.
92. Scott M. Gibson, Preaching to a Shifting Culture (Grand Rapids, MI: Baker Books, 2004), 178.

CHAPTER 4

The Church is Called To Preach

Postmodernists tend to believe that traditional methods of preaching browbeat the listener. Preaching, however, is rather distinct to the Christian faith. In fact, we read in Mark 1:14, Matthew 4:17, and in Luke 4:18 that Christ began his public ministry and claimed to be the fulfiller of Isaiah 61, which states that God anointed and sent Christ to preach the gospel message. Jesus made it clear that when he spoke, it was to proclaim the Word of his Father. Christ said in John 14:10, "the words that I speak unto you I speak not of myself; but the Father that dwell in me, he doeth the works."

The fact is, preaching is a unique divine-human task, which includes humanity's effort and God's Holy Spirit in order to make it victorious. I realize humanity does not have the capability to win the lost on its own, but we can do our part by the power of the Holy Spirit. The Apostle Paul instructed Timothy in 2 Timothy 2:15, "to be a workman who correctly handles the word of truth." 1 Corinthians 3:9 tells us, "... we are laborers together with God." The reality is, we have been commissioned to go into the entire world and preach the Gospel, the Good News of Jesus Christ, which is the Good News for all times.

Preaching is also vital to man's spiritual condition. Unfortunately, many people, as well as church congregations, neglect this spiritual aspect of man's condition. We often hear it said that a person has a mental condition, but it may well be that the individual has a spiritual condition. Martin Lloyd-Jones said in his book, *Preaching and Preachers*, "There are so many people trying to diagnose the human situation; and they come to the conclusion that man is sick, man is unhappy, man is the victim of circumstances...man's real trouble is that he is a rebel against God and consequently under the wrath of God."[93]

True Biblical Preaching

Preaching has one aim: that Christ may come to those who have assembled to listen to the message that he offers us life in the here and now. John R.W. Stott says in his book, *Biblical Preaching Today*, that preaching "has its place in the battle between God and the Devil. The word of the preacher is an attack on the prison in which man is held. It opens the prison, and sets him free."[94]

Preaching aside from Christ is not preaching. Luke 4:18 lays emphasis on the Messiah. Christ was speaking of himself that day as the fulfillment of Isaiah 61:1-2. God the Father sent him and God's Spirit anointed him to preach the good news, which is himself, the long-awaited, much-anticipated Messiah, who came to do mighty works that no one had ever attained or could ever attain: liberate those who needed liberating, release the captives, and deliver those in need of deliverance. 2 Corinthians 3:17 says "Now the Lord is the Spirit: and where the Spirit of the Lord is, there is Liberty."

True biblical preaching has never been dull and boring. In fact, people in Jesus' day often journeyed extreme distances to hear the Word that Christ proclaimed, which was always pertinent and relevant to his audience because he always spoke in terms specific people could relate to. When he addressed farmers, for example, he spoke in terms of farming. When addressing fishermen, Christ spoke in terms of fishing. As Stott explains, "The expository preacher is a bridge builder, seeking to span the gulf between the Word of God and the mind of man."[95]

𝔓𝔯𝔢𝔞𝔠𝔥𝔦𝔫𝔤 𝔞𝔫𝔡 𝔱𝔥𝔢 𝔑𝔢𝔢𝔡𝔰 𝔬𝔣 𝔱𝔥𝔢 ℭ𝔥𝔲𝔯𝔠𝔥

As Lloyd-Jones says, "the primary task of the Church and of the Christian minister is the preaching of the Word of God."[96] He does not mean that preaching is the primary task in all churches but that preaching the Word of God should be the primary task of the church, a statement he biblically validates. In Acts 3, for example, we read that when Peter and John were outside the Temple Beautiful, they prayed for a man who had been lame. The man was raised up, and as a result, the onlookers were drawn by the notable miracle. John and Peter, however, redirected the crowd's attention to Christ and preaching their need for salvation.

In Acts 6 there arose a murmuring of the Grecians against the Hebrews because their widows were neglected in the daily ministration. So the twelve called the multitude of disciples unto them, and said, "it is not reason that we should leave the Word of God, and serve tables." So the church needed to deal with the matter but not at the cost of neglecting the proclamation of God's Word.

In every age, many issues and concerns have arrived on church doorsteps, but those concerns should never become our primary task. I am certainly not suggesting we neglect current situations in life! There is a common saying in the churches that we are so heavenly minded we are no earthly good, but it may be that we, the church, can be so earthly minded that we are no heavenly good.

Christ told the Apostle Peter in John 21:16, "Feed my Sheep." The spiritual feeding and nourishment of God's children is made first part of the great apostolic office. J. C. Ryle says in his book, *Expository Thoughts in the Gospels, volume 4*, "When the Lord said, 'feed' I believe he meant that Peter was to feed souls with the precious food of God's Word, to supply them with that bread of life which a man must eat or die, and to watch carefully and diligently over the spiritual interests, like a good shepherd watching his flock."[97] After all, both the Old Testament and the New Testament say that "Man does not live by bread alone but by every word that proceeds out of the mouth of God."

Let us realize the Apostles sat under the Lord for three-and-a-half years and heard the Word of God. They continued what the Lord had begun by preaching the Word, using the same messages they had heard directly from Christ himself. It was not merely the act of preaching, but the message that made the difference. You will also notice the accounts of Matthew, Mark, Luke, and John often complement each other, yet each Gospel writer recorded the life of Christ from a unique frame of reference. John 20:30-31 says, "Many other signs therefore did Jesus in the presence of the disciples, which are not written in this book, these are written, that ye may believe that Jesus is the Christ, the Son of God; and that believing ye may have life in his name."

The Power of the Word

What makes the Word powerful is the fact that it comes from God himself. When Christ came in the flesh he spoke the words of the Father. Christ stated in John 14:24b, "The word which ye hear is not mine, but the Father's which sent me." Likewise, the Apostles spoke the word of God because they were present with Christ while he was on earth. Christ prayed to God the Father in John 17:8, "for the words which thou gravest me I have given unto them; and they received them, and knew of a truth that I came forth from thee, and they believed that thou didst send me."

The Gospel messages have been tried and tested. There is power in the Word of God because it is inspired and God-breathed. The Bible declares, "Let there be light, and there was light," and we see the correlation between God's Word and the results, for God's Word does not return void, according to Isaiah 55:11: "so shall my word be that goeth forth out of my mouth: it shall not return unto me void, but it shall accomplish that which I please, and it shall prosper in the thing whereto I sent it."

Preaching, therefore, is to proclaim the Word of God, not an opportunity to say what is on your mind or to promote your own agenda. The Word of God is without peer. The result of true preaching is so powerful that people are moved to service in Christ. Hebrews 4:12 says, "For the Word of God is quick and powerful, and sharper than any two-edged sword, piercing even to the dividing asunder of soul and spirit, and of the joints and marrow, and is a discerner of the thought and intents of the heart."

I recall being in a church a few years ago where the minister was preaching on how great a man John the Baptist was. Figuratively speaking, John the Baptist would roll over in his grave if he had heard that message. John was filled with God's Holy Spirit from his mother's womb. His mission and purpose were to proclaim Christ the Messiah and the fact that the kingdom was at hand. The purpose of the scriptures was never to glorify John the Baptist or any other man, but to give glory to God. When the religious leaders of John's day asked him who he was, John tells them in Mark 1:7, "there is one who comes after me is greater than I." The Bible is not about John the Baptist; it's about God and his relationship to humanity.

Effective (and Affective) Spirit-Filled Preaching

Preaching the Word of God affects the lives of those who receive it because the Word of God is divine. Paul writes in Romans 1:16 that the gospel is "the power of God for salvation to everyone who has faith." When the gospel is faithfully proclaimed, the Holy Spirit moves and generates redeeming grace in the hearts of those who believe unto newness of life. This was certainly true in Acts 2. When Peter concluded his famous sermon on the Day of Pentecost, we read, "When they heard this, they were pierced to the heart."

This happens because God is a living Spirit. The same power that affected the lives of people 2000 years ago can have that same effect in the lives of people today. Hebrews 13:8 proclaims, "Jesus Christ is the same yesterday and today, and forever."

Today our great High Priest (Hebrews 4:14) sits at God's right hand just as he did yesterday and does for all eternity. According to Acts 4:12, it is the Lord who has commissioned us (his people, the church) to reach the world with a message of hope found only in Christ, who alone is the Savior of the world.

Teaching Sound Doctrine

We also have a duty to man, as well as God, to teach sound doctrine. The Apostle Paul instructed Titus in Titus 2:1 "You must teach what is in accord with sound doctrine." While Christ was here on earth, this is what he did, but now he has commissioned us to do the same. Christ primarily preached to the lost sheep of Israel but commissioned the Apostles to preach the Gospel to the ends of the earth in Acts 1:8. God has chosen to save the world through the proclamation of the Gospel.

Many religious leaders of Jesus' day believed the Messiah would come with a sword and destroy all of Israel's enemies. However, Christ came into this world to save humanity, not to destroy it. The great commission found in Matthew 28:19-20 and in Romans 10:15 states, "And how shall they preach, except they be sent? As it is written, how beautiful are the feet of them that preach the gospel of peace, and bring glad tidings of good things!"

Preaching in the Postmodern Era

We are living in a day and age where biblical authority is being challenged. This is nothing new, however. In fact, it goes all the way back to Genesis 3, when humanity (original sin) rebelled against God. The Apostle Paul also lived in a day when people challenged his apostolic and scriptural authority. Even in 1886, A.J. Gordon predicted (as quoted in Gibson), "...a day would come when men and women would be led entirely out of the way due to their rebellious position toward the Word of God."[98]

The Bible, however, is inspired by God. It, therefore, has authority and is relevant in every generation. Regardless of any obstacles in this world, whether they originated in the Apostle Paul's day, or in the nineteenth, twentieth, or twenty-first centuries, God's Word remains powerful. Matthew 24:25 says, "Heaven and earth shall pass away, but my words shall not pass away." The Bible is self-authenticating, which means it can stand alone and is not in need of others to defend it. Even though there are difficulties in the lives of humanity, preaching God's Word is the antidote. As believers in Christ, we have a right relationship with God the Father and therefore He has given us full authority and commissioned us to preach the good news of His Son Christ Jesus.

Notes

93. D. Martyn Lloyd-Jones, Preaching and Preachers (Grand Rapids, MI: Zondervan Publishing House, 1972), 27.
94. John R.W. Stott, Biblical Preaching Today (Grand Rapids, MI: William B. Eerdmans Publishing Company, 1961), 108.
95. Ibid., 28.
96. Lloyd-Jones, 19.
97. J. C. Ryle, Expository Thoughts in the Gospels, vol.4 (Grand Rapids, MI: Baker Book House, 2007), 450.
98. Gibson, 215.

CHAPTER 5

The Battle for Winning
Postmodernists to Christ

reaching often touches the emotions of the heart without challenging the intellect. Peter Adam, in his book, *Speaking God's Word*, says, "Our preaching should convey, not reduce, the intellectual and emotional impact of our text."[99] Luke 10:27 also makes this clear: "And He (Christ) answering said, Thou shalt love the Lord thy God with all thy heart, and with all thy soul, and with all thy strength, and with all thy mind." When preaching to the postmodernist, both the heart and mind need to be engaged so that when the postmodernists ask the tough questions, they receive more than superficial answers with which they would not be satisfied.

Many people within the church see postmodernists as hostile to the faith, so they would rather avoid them by avoiding their questions and instead focus on those who agree with them and hold to the same faith. While we should endeavor to answer the questions of the postmodernists, we should also be discerning toward those who are not asking questions about the faith because they think he/she has all the answers. There are also those who are not ready to hear the Word of God because they do not want to believe, so we should be careful not to spend time with them. Matthew 7:6 states, "Give not that which is holy unto the dogs, neither cast ye your pearls before swine, lest they trample them under their feet, and turn again and rend you." Nevertheless, the Christian mission is to win the lost.

The battle of winning the lost is not a new challenge reserved for the postmodernist population. 1 Corinthians 1:22-23 tells us, for example, "for the Jews require a sign, and the Greeks seek after wisdom: but we preach Christ crucified, unto the Jews a stumbling block, and unto the Greeks foolishness." The Jews, as a nation, had seen Old Testament events unfold firsthand and were entrusted with the Holy Scriptures, even though many of them perished due to their unbelief. The Greeks, on the other hand, were men of earthly wisdom who studied culture and sciences and were known for their philosophy and great learning. They did not realize, however, that wisdom is only found in Christ.

The Lord Jesus Christ had a purpose for the Apostle Paul, and that was to present the gospel to all people. Paul was careful not to be a stumbling block to the Gentiles but at the same time never excused himself from complying with the unbelieving Jews, in order to win them to Christ. So, Paul reasoned with philosophers in terms they could understand so they would comprehend the message. When Paul dealt with the Greeks on Mars Hill in Acts 17, for example, he spoke about their unknown god in a manner they would understand.

Paul sums up his approach to proclaiming the gospel of Christ as the salvation of all souls in 1 Corinthians 9:22: "To the weak I became weak, that I might win the weak; I have become all things to all men, so that I may by all means save some." The basic message is the same, however, the purpose of which is that "you may come to believe that Jesus is the Messiah, the Son of God, and through believing you may have life in his name," as John 20:31 says.

Postmodernists tend to believe, however, that truth is determined by the community in which they live. As Stanley J. Grenz writes in his book, *A Primer on Postmodernism*, "Since there are many human communities, there are necessarily many different truths. Most postmodernists make the leap of believing that this plurality of truths can exist alongside one another."[100] We are living in a day where pluralism and tolerance of others' beliefs and opinions are all expected. An example of this was when Rodney King tried to bring about a sense of calm during the 1992 L.A. riots and said on national TV, "Can't we all get along?"

In their desperation to make pluralism work, most postmodernists also believe all religions are the same. Nothing could be further from the truth, however. As Harold Netland writes in his book, *Encountering Religious Pluralism,* "Since each religion typically regards its own beliefs as true, such conflicts produce what is often called the problem of conflicting truth claims."[101]

Pluralism, specifically religious pluralism, actually dates back to when our country was founded as a nation. In the United States, freedom of religion is a guaranteed right provided by the First Amendment of the Constitution. This was one of the attractions of America for those who left their counties to escape political persecution. However, this is also why the United States has such an emphasis on the plurality of faiths and non-faiths. Unfortunately, says Grenz, "Most postmoderns make the leap of believing that this plurality of truths can exist alongside one another. The postmodern consciousness, therefore, entails a radical kind of relativism and pluralism."[102]

Postmodernism ideology has also slipped into the church. A common question Bible study leaders ask their groups is "What does the passage mean to you?" Rather than determining that the Word of God is true, even our Bible study leaders are encouraging those studying under them to determine truth, whether they realize it or not. R. Scott Smith says in his book, *Truth and the New Kind of Christian,* "Christians are increasingly accepting of ethical relativism, and in a climate that promotes pluralism, we are losing our understanding of Christian ethical and religious truths as being objectively true."[103]

No matter who you are or which religion you adhere to, truth is something we all desire. It is most difficult to live our lives without certainty. Most people can live with truth, but not uncertainty. Even the supporters of pluralism require truth because the truth is liberating. Christ said in John 8:32, "You will know the truth, and the truth will set you free." Without truth, we would have every reason to be despondent. Truth is also comforting. Even though postmodernists claim they do not believe in absolute truth, they are looking for it.

Religion and Postmodernists

Postmodernists believe all religions are the same and that all roads lead to heaven because they want a life of peace. However, as much as they want to believe we can all just "get along," there are just too many significant differences between religions. Before 911, for example, most Americans did not know who Muslims were or what they believed, so it was easy for postmodernists to say that all religions are the truth.

According to the Islam religion, however, there is only one god, whose name is Allah. Christians also believe there is only one God, but Islam rejects the Trinity, the incarnation, and the resurrection. Other areas where the two religions differ are Isaac and Ishmael, the creation account, Christ and the miracles he performed, and how to treat enemies. Postmodernists also believe Christianity and Buddhism are alike, but Christianity is based on the teachings of the person Jesus Christ. Buddha was a man in search of the truth. At this point, hopefully, we can see that saying all religions are the same is an uneducated and ridicules notion.

Authority and the Faith

We have probably all seen the bumper sticker that says "Question Authority." At one time, this would have been viewed as a radical thought. However, the scandals involving priests and pastors, the IRS, and Benghazi where four Americans were killed, have given postmodernists fuel for their skepticism. For many years, individuals respected the church, the government, and others in positions of authority, but as Gary G. Cohen reports in *Biblical Decision Making, Intelligent Design, and Creation:* "The post-modern generation has lost faith in the experts. This loss of faith extends to world leaders, scientists, and theologians because the post-modern generation has heard so many palpably credible and plausible conflicting opinions, they know somebody must be wrong, if not everybody."[104]

For postmodernists, nothing is sacred, for even God and the Bible are under scrutiny. Instead, they put their trust in the theory of humanities, yet reject human scholarship and at times, science. Johnston says that "Postmodernity comes with a generation that has grown up in broken homes, been lied to by politicians, and often deceived by the church and community leaders. The church makes bold claims but rarely delivers on its own message of love, reconciliation, and compassion."[105] Whether the church agrees with the experiences and position of the postmodernists, these are real concerns the church needs to address, so it is not misunderstood and misrepresented.

The church needs to reassess itself because it is losing members. The 2009 Barna Group Report, which examines the state of mainline protestant churches, reports "In the past fifty years, mainline church membership dropped by more than one-quarter to roughly 20 million people. Adult church attendance indicates that only 15% of all American adults associate with a mainline church these days."[106]

As a result, churches have turned to a more postmodernist approach by becoming seeker friendly, which often leads to toning down the biblical messages for fear of being offensive. Unfortunately, as Haddon W. Robinson says in the book, *Preaching to a Shifting Culture*, "Too much of current preaching resembles cotton candy that appeals to people's hunger but possesses no value as food."[107] However, since attendance is down, churches are attempting to reinvent themselves.

Churches have often gone to great expense in taking down their historical denominational signs so individuals will think of the church as being fashionably non-denominational. Some churches have even done away with the pulpit. The pastor will wear jeans rather than a suit so that others will see the pastor as approachable. Unfortunately, it also gives the appearance of someone who is not in authority.

Churches have even changed their music to a mix of liturgy and rock bands, complete with gourmet coffee and bagels. Many churches are holding separate services: one that features traditional worship music, and one that features contemporary. These external changes are all in a desperate attempt to attract people. Gundry fears, however, that (as quoted in Craig Bartholomew, Robin Parry, and Andrew West's book, *The Future of Evangelism*) "that evangelicals have lost their fundamentalist edge, that they are no longer opposed to worldliness but in bed with it."[108]

Authority of Scripture

I was a professor for a number of years at a Bible university. When my students gave a reason for their beliefs, it was often based on their denominational beliefs or the beliefs of their pastor, but not necessarily on the Word of God. This is because students were often aware of their denominational beliefs but unaware of what the scriptures read. This led students to believe their churches may have held different views from the Bible. A pastor will often read his notes or outline from an open Bible, giving the thought that what the pastor is saying is being read from the inspired Word of God. This is a deception on the pastor's part, whether intentional or unintentional.

Many students also held a low view of scripture. A common question I received was, "Why are there so many interpretations of the Bible?" The answer I often gave was that they were probably reading or hearing commentary and not the scriptures.

I remember a student objecting to something I had said during class. He said, "My Bible reads differently." I said, "I would love to see it!" He pointed to a page in his Bible, but it was the commentary and not the inspired Word of God. I realize that commentaries can be quite helpful as they pertain to history, archeology, customs, and so forth, but I found the students did not know the difference between the commentaries and God's Word. As a result, I found the Word of God had little impact on their lives.

The traditions of men have again taken precedence over the Word of God, just as the traditions of the Jewish people did in Jesus' time. Jesus made it clear in Matthew 15:1-6 that the Jews worshiped in vain and nullified the Word of God because they held to their traditions instead of obeying God's commandments. That is why Jesus said in Matthew 15:6b, "Thus have ye made the commandment of God of none effect by your tradition." When Christ dealt with this type of situation in Matthew, he said in verse 5:22, "you have heard it said… but I say unto you …." So Christ confronted them with the transgression of the traditions of men and exalted God's divine Word as the only rule of faith and practice. Religion had so elevated their customs that they had overturned the Word of God. To deprive the inspired scriptures is to deprive God's Word of its authority and render it void. This is often the reason the lives of postmodernists have little transformation.

As a professor I found myself spending my first class building on the foundation that the Word of God is and continues to be the ultimate authority, using the words of the Apostle Paul in 2 Timothy 3:16, "All scripture is given by inspiration of God." Postmodernists often consider this an enormous statement, but we need to be mindful of the challenge the Lord has sent out to those refusing to acknowledge Him as Lord and creator of all. In Isaiah 40:25-26, we read, "To whom then will you compare me, or who is equal? Says the Holy One. Lift up your eyes upon high and see: Who created these?"

The Lord himself gives the answer in Isaiah 42:5. He is the one "who created the heavens and stretched them out, who spread out the earth and what comes from it." These statements make it clear that God alone is the sole creator of all things. Believing in the reality of God is a stretch for postmodernists, however, and they would rather hold to the atheistic or at least the agnostic belief.

Authority of Pop Culture

Unlike any other time in history, we are bombarded with information. News of events can be viewed 24/7, and many opinions by commentators have come into our homes. It is interesting to see how the vast majority of the public question authority yet value the opinions of people who have no true insight and authority in the things of God, such as William "Bill" Maher, Jr., for example, an American stand-up comedian, television host, political commentator, author, and actor. While he holds a B.A. in English and history from Cornell University, he is not an authority on Scripture. The postmodern world, however, looks at him and others like him as if they are the true authorities on religion.

When someone does speak from a position of authority, the postmodernists believe that a person is entitled to his or her opinion and they are entitled to theirs. Johnston says that "Postmodernity is a consumer age, where people will relish options. Plurality demands these options in which all choices share equal footing. Because there is no center, no clear target, there exists a need for a variety of possibilities on the parameter of life."[109] As a result, postmodernists have come to believe they are right in their own eyes just as the Jews did in the book of Judges. Judges 21:25 famously declares "everyone did [does] what is right in their own eyes." The postmodernist does not realize; however, this is resulting from the fall of humanity, for it was Adam's sin that broke fellowship and communion with God. Consequently, we read in Isaiah 59:2 that "Your iniquities have separated between you and your God, and your sins have hid his face from you, so that he will not hear."

This is where the great divide comes in between the postmodernist and a believer. The believer knows he or she is not independent of his or her creator and sits under the authority of God and his Word. A Christian believes it is God who determines good and evil, whereas the unbeliever has "become like gods," determining what is good and what is evil. The Word of God needs to be brought to the forefront as the authority to the postmodernist world. The Apostle Peter references the Apostle Paul with this warning in 2 Peter 3:16-17: "His letters contain some things that are hard to understand, which ignorant and unstable people distort, as they do the other Scriptures to their own destruction. Therefore; dear friends, since you already know this, be on your guard so that you may not be carried away by the error of lawless men and fall from your secure position."

The bottom line is that postmodernists need to be reached with God's Truth. To understand the postmodernists the preacher will realize they are suspicious of faith and truth but can be reached with the Gospel message if it is presented in such a way that Christianity is both reasonable and plausible. According to Geisler and Turek, "The Law of Excluded Middle tells us that something is or is not. For example, either God exists or he does not. Either Jesus rose from the dead or he did not. There are no third alternatives."[110]

ꟼotes

99. Peter Adam, Speaking God's Word (Vancouver, BC: Regent College Publishing, 1996), 97.

100. Stanley J. Grenz, A Primer on Postmodernism (Grand Rapids, MI; William B. Eerdmans Publishing Company, 1996), 14.

101. Harold Netland, Encountering Religious Pluralism (Downers Grove, IL: IVP Academic, 2001), 181.

102. Grenz, 14.

103. R. Scott Smith, Truth and the New Kind of Christian (Wheaton, IL: Crossway Books, 2005), 13.

104. Gary G. Cohen, Biblical Decision Making, Intelligent Design, and Creation (Eugene, OR: Wipf and Stock Publishers, 2006), 13.

105. Johnston, 55.

106. Barna Group, American Christians Do Not Believe that Satan or the Holy Spirit Exist, last modified April 10, 2009, accessed December 5, 2013, https://www.barna.org/barna-update/article/12-faithspirituality/260-most-american-christians-do-not-believe-that-satan-or-the-holy-spirit-exis#.UwlNTjYo5D8

107. Haddon W. Robinson, Preaching to a Shifting Culture, ed. Scott M. Gibson (Grand Rapids, MI: Baker Books, 2004), 82.

108. Craig Bartholomew, Robin Parry, & Andrew West, The Future of Evangelicalism (Grand Rapids, MI: Kregel, 2003), 43.

109. Johnston, 39.

110. Geisler & Turek, 62.

CHAPTER 6

Preaching To Save and to Mature

Preaching to the postmodernists comes from a legitimate concern that many are not being reached with the gospel message, which must be presented in such a way that the soul is delighted with the message, using rhetoric for stylistic purposes and apologetics for substantive content. Combining the Word of God with rhetoric and an explanation of the logic of the Word will move the postmodernist toward the truth. According to Cicero (as quoted in Herrick), "Rhetoric's great power is useful only when tempered by great wisdom."[111]

Even those who actually accept the Bible as carrying unique authority rather than putting it on the same playing field with Koran, the Vedas, or the Talmud, might say, "That's your interpretation, not mine!"[112] This is why apologetics is necessary because many postmodernists view the Christian faith as unproven and defying the laws of reason and logic. According to Robertson McQuilkin in his book, *Understanding and Applying the Bible*, "If it is God's Word, revealing His will, nothing could be of greater importance than understanding it. If the Bible was given to reveal the truth and not to hide it, God must intend that we understand it. If we do not, the fault must lie with us, not with Him."[113] Johnston reminds us that "God's truth transcends culture; for God's truth to penetrate today's culture we have only to find ways to bridge the biblical and the postmodern worlds--to speak meaningfully to people where they are."[114]

Postmodernists will not believe unless they can be convinced the Bible is the inspired, inerrant, and authoritative Word of the living God. Preaching to the postmodernist, therefore, should always strive to give understanding that brings glory to God by highlighting the meaning and relevance of the biblical text. The Word of God is to be spoken as biblically solid and theologically sound messages, which speak and stir the hearts of the people, as it pertains to our present reality.

Preaching that is Expository

Part of the problem is that the church and the pulpit are often not used to further the kingdom of God, nor do they have a theocentric focus. Instead, they are often used as platforms for politics, civil rights, and social movements of every other sort. However, if we are preaching the Bible in an expository manner, Merrill Unger in his book, *The Modern Preaching*, says we succeed in "... handling the text in such a way that its real and essential meaning as it existed in the mind of the particular Biblical writer and as it exists in the light of the overall context of Scripture is made plain and applied to the present-day needs of the hearers."[115]

As Bryan Chapel says in his book, *Christ-Centered Preaching*, the result is "Preaching that is true to Scripture converts, convicts, and eternally changes the souls of men and women because God's Word is the instrument of divine compulsion."[116] In fact, preaching the gospel message is the way Jesus began his public ministry, according to Mark 1:14-15: "The time is fulfilled, and the kingdom of God is at hand: repent ye, and believe the gospel." He also said in Luke 4:43, "I must preach the good news of the kingdom of God to the other towns also, because that is why I was sent." So Christ proclaimed the Good News throughout his entire ministry. Christ's final words before leaving this earth in Mark 16:15 gave the "great commission" for His apostles to, "Go into all the world, and preach the gospel to every creature." Not stopping there, the Apostle Paul instructed Timothy to preach the Word as an ongoing mission for him as well as a mission for the church.

Today, as Christ's representative, R. Alan Street says in his book, *The Effective Invitation*, that a preacher "has divine authority and, therefore, has the right to be heard."[117] P.T. Forsyth, as quoted in Richard Lischer's book, *Theories of Preaching*, distinguishes the difference between Greek oratory of the Apostle Paul's day and preaching: "Preaching is the most distinct institution in Christianity. It is quite different from oratory.... The Christian preacher is not the successor of the Greek orator, but of the Hebrew Prophet. The orator comes with but an inspiration, the prophet with a revelation."[118]

C. H. Dodd makes clear in his book *The Apostolic Preaching* that preaching (*kerygma*) is the proclamation of the death, burial, and resurrection of Christ directed toward the non-Christian world, while teaching (*didaskein*) was directed toward the Christians, those who were already believers, so they would be encouraged, exhorted, and directed to live a moral life in the body of Christ. Dodd says, "... wherever 'Preaching' is spoken of, it always carries with it the implications of 'good tidings' proclaimed."[119]

With all this in mind, true Christian preaching is expository, so not everyone who stands behind the pulpit is preaching. Gibson, ed. says, "...expository preaching...is biblical preaching [of] the most relevant message we can offer to our hearers.... it is preaching that draws its substance from the Scriptures."[120] Christ and his Word are inseparable, for Christ remains active in his Word. Unfortunately for many listeners, many contemporary preachers prefer to tell their own stories, having little or any spiritual impact on their congregations, who are often left uncertain and puzzled wondering whether he/she has heard Godly wisdom or just the pastor's opinion. All too often people who attend church do not hear the inspired Word of God and are left instead with a denominational teaching. In 1 Thessalonians 2:13, however, the Apostle Paul commends the Thessalonian church for accepting the message "not as the word of men, but as it actually is, the word of God, which is at work in you who believe."

Christ defined what preaching was in John 20:21b when he said, "as the Father hath sent me, even so send I you," and continued in John 14:31 with "The word which ye hear is not mine, but the Fathers who sent me." So it should be today; the scriptures declare that "Whoever speaks must do so as one speaking the very words of God...so that God may be glorified in all things through Jesus Christ." (1 Peter 4:11).

The body of Christ needs solid biblical teaching to build up the body and be able to speak to the postmodern population. 2 Timothy 3:16-17 says, "All scripture is given by inspiration of God, and is profitable for doctrine, for reproof, for correction, for instruction in righteousness: That the man of God may be perfect, thoroughly furnished unto all good works." So as Norman Geisler and William E. Nix contend in their book, *A General Introduction to the Bible*, "... the Scriptures are profitable because they are inspired."[121]

Preaching that is Deep and Meaningful

"Preaching Christ" is often restricted to preaching Christ's death, burial, and resurrection. While the message of the cross is necessary and essential for salvation, for many, the message ends there. According to Sidney Greidanus, author of *Preaching Christ from the Old Testament*, "... to preach Christ is to proclaim some facet of the person, work, or teaching of Jesus of Nazareth so that the people may believe him, trust him, love him, and obey him."[122]

Hebrews 6:1-2 says, "Therefore leaving the principles of the Doctrine of Christ, let us go on unto perfection; not laying again the foundation of repentance from dead works, and of faith toward God. Of the doctrine of Baptisms, and of the Laying on of hands, and of resurrection of the dead, and eternal judgment." The church must, therefore, pursue developing the foundation of individuals to grow and mature beyond salvation so they will advance their growth in the Word of God and be able to reach the postmodern population instead of remaining in the infant stage of Christianity.

Postmodernists need to receive satisfactory answers to the questions they have, so for the church to be built up, grow, and develop, it is necessary, as the writer of Hebrews states, for us to "go on." The problem is that since we have many people in our churches who are skeptical of the message, they never develop a solid foundation, to begin with from which to mature. Christ never wanted anyone to remain in that state; He wanted all Christians to mature so they could be effective in the body of Christ. Unfortunately, their growth is stopping prematurely because they are weak and malnourished. In that state, such individuals are unable to reach the postmodernists because they are unable to provide satisfactory answers to their questions.

As I have stated, maturity begins with a solid foundation, which is illustrated in the parable of the wise and foolish builders in Matthew 7:24-27: "Therefore everyone who hears these words of mine and puts them into practice is like a wise man who built his house on the rock. The rain came down, the streams rose, and the winds blew and beat against the house; yet it did not fall, because it had its foundation on the rock. But everyone who hears these words of mine and does not put them into practice is like a foolish man who built his house on sand. The rain came down, the streams rose, and the winds blew and beat against the house, and it fell with a great crash."

The parable contrasts two men building a house. The foolish person builds his house on a poor foundation (sand), which means he may hear the Word of God but not put it into practice. The wise man builds upon a solid (rock) foundation, meaning he heard the Word of God and put it into practice.

Biblically and practically, all Christians need a solid foundation from which to mature. Almost every year here in California, we hear about homes that have not been built on a solid foundation and are washed away during the rainy season. Similarly, the Bible speaks of God or Christ as the "rock," the only true foundation, which is also found in Genesis 49:24, Psalm 18:2, and 1 Corinthians 10:4. It is in Him (Christ) that we are told to lay our solid foundation.

Often we hear of people being disappointed by their evangelists, pastors, priests, and other Christians, so they leave the church or leave their faith. People let us down; having said that our faith should not be in a person or an institution, but in no one else but Christ, who is the rock of our salvation. Trusting in anything or anyone else is sinking sand.

Preaching Beyond the Cross

While preaching on the death, burial and resurrection is essential and a solid foundation from which to build, the excitement and the energy of preaching needs to go beyond the cross. In Mark 1:1 we read that Christ's ministry was explosive and exciting: 'The beginning of the good news of Jesus Christ, the son of God," the good news being that the Messiah forgives sin and has come to introduce his kingdom rule to the world. This was the Messianic Kingdom that John the Baptist prepared his people for, as prophesied in Isaiah 40:3.

John's appearance, along with his ascetic lifestyle, spoke like the prophet of old and created so much excitement among the Jews that in John 1:19 we read, "The Jews of Jerusalem sent priests and Levites to ask him who he was. John the Baptizer, did not fail to confess, but confessed freely, 'I am not the Christ.'" In fact, John declares that in comparison to the one who is to come, his "... sandals I am not worthy to untie." For the Christ is not just an anointed one, but the Messiah. God penned Isaiah 52:6-7 through his prophet approximately 700 years before the Messiah came to earth: "How beautiful upon the mountains are the feet of the messenger who announces peace, who brings good news, who announces salvation, who says to Zion." Isaiah also described what would become the Messiah's activity Isaiah 60:1, which was fulfilled in Luke 4:21: "And there was delivered unto him the book of the Prophet Isaiah. And he opened the book, and found the place where it was written, The Spirit of the Lord is upon me, Because he anointed me to preach good tidings to the poor: He hath sent me to proclaim release to the captives, And recovering of sight to the blind, To set at liberty them that are bruised, And he began to say unto them, To-day hath this scripture been fulfilled in your ears." This is the good news the world had been waiting for! So there was great anticipation and expectation of the Lord, an excitement echoed by John the Baptist who stated, "The kingdom of God was at hand."

When Christ came, the Messiah demonstrated his authority by casting out demons, healing the sick, and cleansing the lepers. He could rightfully declare, "the Kingdom of God has come upon you." Before their very eyes, hope became a reality. As James S. Stewart said in his book, *Heralds of God*, "No longer were they dreaming of the Kingdom age: they were living in it; it had arrived."[123] Not only did Christ have a victorious entrance as He began His ministry, but people revered Him. The next day, John the Baptist introduced Him to the world in John 1:29 as, "… the Lamb of God which take away the sin of the world." Jesus Christ, (the Messiah) was no ordinary man and needed to be preached in such a way that this message was clear. As Loscalzo declares in his book *Evangelistic Preaching*, "Jesus, with his life and ministry, brought the presence of God from heaven to earth. The incarnation reminds us that God is not a distant landlord, uninterested in the world. In Jesus Christ, God became a human player in human history."[124]

When Christ came to earth and became flesh, that meant he was not a god someone could have made up, but he was, as John 1:14 says, "the Word made flesh who dwelt among us." Christ goes even further by saying, "you see me you see the Father." He is more than a concept or a made-up belief. Any religion can make something up, but Christ was from the beginning as we read in John 1:1. He is not only a biblical figure who can be substantiated but historically supported. Christ not only proclaimed himself to be the truth in John 14, but he also came as the revealer of truth, as Lischer says: "The revelation of God came originally in the event of Jesus of Nazareth preaching himself as the revelation of God."[125]

The grand inauguration in time happened in Luke 3:22 when Jesus was baptized in the river Jordan: "and the Holy Spirit descended in a bodily form, as a dove, upon him, and a voice came out of heaven, Thou art my beloved Son: in thee I am well pleased." No doubt it was for all those to witness by hearing and seeing. Luther writes about Christ, "Here he begins rightly to be the Christ," namely the Anointed One, "and was thus inaugurated into his entire Messianic office as our Prophet, High Priest, and King."

After Christ's inauguration, Dunn-Wilson writes, "He comes into Galilee preaching the Gospel of God. So that the people first encounter him as a preacher. Later congregations come to understand that Jesus is no ordinary preacher but the One whose 'proclamation of the good news' brings universal peace and opens the way to God."[126] Mark repeatedly uses the word *astonished* or *astonishment* to describe Christ's teaching. In Mark 6:2 he says, "They were astonished at his teaching, they were all amazed, and they all kept on asking one another, 'What is this?'" This is exhilarating. This is the excitement of God's scripture that we have lost in preaching. Now we are only left with preaching comprised of uninspired stories that are not from the Bible. In order to impact the lives of individuals, it is necessary to use the inspired Word.

Preaching that is Filled with the Spirit's Power

We meet the Spirit of God in the first words of the Bible, and in its opening sentences in Genesis 1: "The Spirit of God moved upon the face of the waters." Says William Barclay in his book, *The Promises of the Spirit*, "The Spirit is the agent of God in creation…. It is the Spirit of God who brings existence out of nothingness, order out of chaos, and beauty out of formlessness."[127]

The Holy Spirit has always played a vital, primary role in the men of God. Whenever the Lord gave a person a task he could not accomplish without God, the Holy Spirit (or God's presence) was always with him. The Lord gave Moses the supernatural ability to part the Red Sea, Samson supernatural strength, Solomon supernatural wisdom the world had never seen, and anointed King David mightily for service in 1 Samuel 16:13: "the Spirit of the Lord came mightily upon David." Humanity could never accomplish supernaturally powerful tasks for God without His presence. So it is with preaching. It is the Lord who provides the power to perform the task.

Acts 1:8 reveals the key powerful preaching: wait until the Holy Spirit has come upon you. Then you shall receive power, and you will be witnesses unto the Lord. Then and now, God's power, (*dynamis* power), His Holy Spirit, was and is necessary for preachers to stand boldly in the face of persecution as they proclaim the Messiah in Acts 4:8, 31, and 6:10. Barclay says, "No man, not even the Son of God, can do God's work without God's Spirit."[128]

On the day of Pentecost, the Holy Spirit was poured out in great abundance, and the apostles (Christ's first preachers) received that power. Wayne Grudem says in his book *Systematic Theology*: "Because the immediate context of the sentence talks about being witnesses for Jesus, they may also have understood him to mean that they would receive power of the Holy Spirit to work through their preaching and bring conviction of sins and awaken faith in people's hearts. This power in their preaching was evident in subsequent events, as when Peter's hearers 'were cut to the heart' (Acts 2:37), or when 'many of those who heard the word believed; and the number of the men came to about five thousand.'"[129]

The impact of apostolic preaching was remarkable as many received Christ and freely accepted him as Lord and Savior. The Holy Spirit works in the lives of the preachers and the hearers because God is in the midst of his people. This assists the hearers in understanding the Word as it is being proclaimed, convicting and comforting. Loscalzo says in his book *Evangelistic Preaching that Connects*, "In every gathering there are probably those who have never responded in any way to the gospel. The illuminating power of the Holy Spirit enables people to understand the truth as it is proclaimed. The Holy Spirit convicts of sin, calls people to Christ, and effects regeneration."[130]

Even Christ's ministry did not begin until the Holy Spirit had come upon him. Before that happened, no recorded wise words and no miracles had occurred. Christ himself said in John 10:38 that "God anointed Him with the Holy Spirit and with power." After Christ was baptized in the river Jordan, he spent some time being tempted by Satan in the wilderness, but when he came out, the scriptures declare that "he came out in the power of the Spirit." The Apostles needed that same supernatural power of the Holy Spirit to accomplish the great commission and were instructed not to go until the Holy Spirit had come upon them.

Fact is, throughout scripture, ever since the fall of man in Genesis 3, humanity is forever in some type of situation he needs God to supernaturally intervene in, resulting in God's glory being made manifest. Humanity was never created to operate independently of God, for man was made in the likeness and image of God. However, the fall corrupted and polluted God's creation, and man has been trying to distance himself from God ever since. Man attempted to cover his nakedness, but he has never been able to rescue himself and still requires a Savior. That is why God has to provide the covering, both then and now. Christ makes a bold proclamation in John 15:5: "without me you can do nothing." A sobering statement.

Preaching that has a Supernatural View

Unfortunately, postmodernists may not believe the creation account, or the stories of Noah, Jonah, Abraham, or the Exodus. Instead, they look through the lens of the natural and do not view God or the Bible from the supernatural perspective. In the natural, God speaking the world into existence sounds bizarre. For the Christian, however, the simple but clear and obvious explanation is that there must be a God and a creator of the entire universe. Whether we view it from a nonbeliever's or a believer's perspective, we must conclude that if the creation account is true, a supernatural power must exist. According to Geisler and Turek, "If Genesis 1:1 is true, 'In the beginning, God created the heavens and the earth,' then every other miracle in the Bible is easy to believe."[131]

Postmodernists will also argue that men wrote the Bible, though they may not have examined it enough to arrive at a rock-solid conclusion. Many postmodernists may be more agnostic than atheistic. Also, some postmodernists do not have any true biblical knowledge of the Christian faith, but rather rely on what he/she has heard. Many postmodernists simply do not know who or what to believe because so many religions claim to be the truth.

Of course, this could be settled if the Christian was capable of explaining that the Bible is both human and divine and is a result of dual authorship. If the matter of the authority and trustworthiness of the scripture is not settled, it is very difficult for postmodernists to value the Christian perspective. The Word does show how scripture is divine, as the phrase "Word of the Lord" shows up nearly five hundred times. The preacher must be able to preach the Gospel message clearly and effectively.

Even the majority of postmodernists in the church don't believe in an absolute truth according to a 1994 report from the Barna research and polling association, which (as cited in Johnston), "...shows that a startling 62 percent of born-again Christians, not just church-goers, say they don't believe in the existence of absolute truth. Interestingly, Barna's national poll of the wider community revealed even more people (closer to 75 percent) reject the notion of absolute truth."[132] Perhaps "truth" is one of those words that has been overused and as a result has lost its meaning.

There was a time in our history when man was taken at his word. Today, however, attorneys are hired to draw up contracts to make people honor their promises, partly because many, including postmodernists, simply no longer take people at their word. Society, in general, has simply moved toward not telling the truth. This is pretty evident in today's commercials, which are solely driven to get us to buy something we may or may not want or need. Then when we purchase these allegedly life-changing products, they often fall short of the results we saw the products get in the commercials. Politicians are also known to make many empty promises and simply do not tell the truth.

For postmodernists, therefore, "truth" has become highly

overrated. For them, the truth cannot be known nor will ever be known. Instead, they believe we should respect all religions and all points of view, and be tolerant of all beliefs because "all roads lead to heaven." Stott writes, however, "… the scriptures declare something radically contradictory when it comes to God and His Word, and that is, "it is impossible for God to lie," (Hebrews 6:18)."[133]

This is what Christ came preaching -- the completely truthful, incapable of lying, Word of God. Christ was and is God's good news for all humanity, and throughout scripture, people have recognized this. Matthew 8, for example, tells the story of a man who had a servant that was at the point of death. Matthew 8:5 begins, "And when he was entered into Capernaum, there came unto him a centurion, beseeching him saying, Lord, my servant lieth in the house sick of the palsy, grievously tormented. And he saith unto him, I will come and heal him." This centurion was clearly aware of who Jesus was and treated him with great respect and honor, not as merely the son of a carpenter, but as Lord. The story is even more interesting considering the centurion was a Gentile, not a Jew. Nevertheless, he is a man who recognizes and understands authority because, as he says in Luke 7:6, "For I also am a man under authority, having under myself soldiers: and I say to this one, Go, and he goeth; and to another, Come, and he cometh; and to my servant, Do this, and he doeth it." Perhaps he had witnessed or heard about the ministry of Christ, the one in whom all power resides, the one who has all power over all things at his very command. So the Centurion said, "Just speak the word." Perhaps he figured if Christ could speak the world into existence, by the power of his Word, he could heal his servant.

Christ came "to destroy the works of the devil." Israel was looking for a King (the Messiah) who would overthrow Israel's enemies and destroy them with the sword. Christ said in Matthew 12:28, "But if I by the Spirit of God cast out demons, then is the kingdom of God come upon you." However, instead of coming with a sword, the Messiah came with the sword of truth in his mouth. Christ came preaching the long-awaited deliverer found in his own Gospel. That is why the writer of Hebrews in 4:12 penned, "The Word of God is quick and powerful sharper than any two-edged sword," and Zechariah 4:6 says, "it is not by might or by strength but by My Spirit."

We have underestimated the power of God in preaching, unlike Paul who declared in Romans 1:16, "For I am not ashamed of the gospel: for it is the power of God unto salvation to everyone that believeth," and the angel who said in Luke 2:10, "I am bringing you good news of great joy for all the people."

In Exodus God's people were in every type of bondage, yet God came to deliver them. Throughout scripture, God has delivered his people. That is why he said, "Let my people go." Even when the Pharaoh refused, God still delivered his people by the power of His Word and man's obedience to it.

Humanity needs help that is beyond himself. All natural resources are inadequate. Ephesians 3:20 says, "Now unto him that is able to do exceeding abundantly above all that we ask or think, according to the power that worketh in us." Sermons need to look beyond heaven and the "sweet by and by" to the fact that Christ came so we could live a life of liberty today. The preacher's sermon should emphasize how Christ can help us live our lives here on earth. This way the Gospel is kept alive through preaching.

Preaching that Reaches the Whole Person

The Lord has made us in such a way that preaching needs to address the whole person. Thomas R. Swears says in his book *Preaching to Head and Heart*, "Christian preaching often does one thing at the expense of another. It addresses the head but doesn't touch the heart. Or, it moves the heart without challenging the mind. Either way, it is less than it could be because it is not addressing the whole person."[134] Anthony A. Hoekema, the author of *Created in God's Image*, continues the thought with "Preaching that merely communicates intellectual information about God or the Bible is seriously inadequate; hearers must be stirred in their hearts and moved to praise God."[135]

Luke 10:27 and Deuteronomy 6:50 make clear that we are to "… love the Lord thy God with all thy heart, and with all thy soul, and with all thy strength, and with all thy mind." We should be preaching the messages of God in such a way that they speak to the heart and penetrate the soul so that they capture and challenge the mind. Ultimately, God desires that those he created love completely and totally and absolutely rest in him. D. Edmond Hiebert says in his book, *Mark: A Portrait of the Servant*, that "Love to God must possess the whole heart, the seat of the personality, the whole soul, the self-conscious life, the whole mind, the rational faculties, and the whole strength, the entire active powers of man."[136] Chappell states, "Preaching that is true to scripture converts, convicts, and eternally changes the souls of men and women."[137]

The bottom line is that God has given us a mind, soul, and body. This is why preaching needs to be delivered using rhetoric and apologetics, to speak to both the head and the heart. According to Grenz, "Knowledge cannot be merely objective, says the postmodernist, because the universe is not mechanistic and dualistic but rather historical, relational, and personal. The world is not simply an objective given that is 'out there,' waiting to be discovered, and known reality is relative, indeterminate, and participatory."[138] By preaching using both rhetoric and apologetics, the listener realizes who he is (human) at the same time he realizes who God is.

Notes

111. Herrick, 102.
112. Johnston, 30.
113. Robertson McQuilkin, Understanding and Applying the Bible (Chicago, IL: Moody Press, 1992), 15.
114. Johnston, 10.
115. Merrill Unger, The Modern Preacher, Principles of Expository Preaching (Grand Rapids, MI: Zondervan, 1955), 33.
116. Bryan Chapel, Christ-Centered Preaching (Grand Rapids, MI: Baker Academic, 2005), 27.

117. R. Alan Streett, The Effective Invitation (Grand Rapids, MI: Kregel Academic and Professional, 1984), 26.

118. Theories of Preaching, 75.

119. C. H. Dodd, The Apostolic Preaching (New York, NY: Harper & Row Publishers, 1964), 8.

120. Scott M. Gibson ed., Preaching to a Shifting Culture (Grand Rapids, MI: Baker Books, 2004), 82.

121. C. H. Dodd, The Apostolic Preaching (New York, NY: Harper & Row Publishers, 1964), 8.

122. Scott M. Gibson ed., Preaching to a Shifting Culture (Grand Rapids, MI: Baker Books, 2004), 82.

123. James S. Stewart, Heralds of God (New York, NY: Charles Scribner's Sons, 1946), 64.

124. Craig A. Loscalzo, Evangelistic Preaching (Downers Grove, IL: InterVarsity Press, 1995), 15.

125. Theories of Preaching, 35.

126. Dunn-Wilson, 23.

127. William Barclay, The Promise of the Spirit (Philadelphia, PA: The Westminister Press, 1960), 12.

128. Barclay, 23.

129. Wayne Grudem, Systematic Theology (Grand Rapids, MI: Zondervan Publishing House, 1994), 638.

130. Craig A. Loscalzo, Evangelistic Preaching that Connects (Downers Grove, IL: InterVarsity Press, 1995) 17.

131. Geisler & Turek. 203.

132. Johnston, 16.

133. John Stott, Evangelical Truth (Downers Grove, IL: InterVarsity Press, 1999), 45.

134. Thomas R. Swears, Preaching to Head and Heart (Nashville, TN: Abingdon Press, 2000), 18.

135. Anthony A. Hoekema, Created in God's Image (Grand Rapids, MI: William B. Eerdmans Publishing Company, 1986), 223.

136. D. Edmond Hiebert, Mark: A Portrait of the Servant (Chicago, IL: Moody Press), 1974), 304.

137. Bryan Chapell, Christ-Centered Preaching (Grand Rapids, MI: Baker Academic, 2005), 27.

138. Grenz, 7.

CHAPTER 7

Don't Resort to Worldly Gimmicks

After I completed this book, I realized postmodernists were more than just a small, fringe group of people; according to the Barna Group, they actually encompass two-thirds of the United States population.[139] What is even more surprising is the fact that the number of postmodernists in our churches is huge. The church, however, is generally not aware of this. The church does, however, seem to be attempting to find new methods of delivering the Gospel message.

I have noticed the church is struggling to find ways to bring the Gospel message forward without using all kinds of incentives and worldly approaches to draw individuals to the church. This accomplishes little in reaching postmodernists, or anyone else for that matter, with the Gospel message. Instead, the focus of the preacher is on personal stories and not the power of the Word of God, as seen historically in the apostles' writing.

Unfortunately, Stott states (as quoted in Nathan Creitz's *Against Preaching: Preaching In A Media-Saturated Culture*), "the prophets of doom in today's Church are confidently predicting that the day of preaching is over. It is a dying art, they say, an outmoded form of communication, an echo from an abandoned past."[140] I believe churches are closing not because the day of preaching is over but because preachers are not preaching the Word of God. This has led to the Spirit of God not being present which has resulted in the Spirit of God not being present

This book also looked back to the history of the church and saw how effective preaching, rhetoric, and apologetics were used. This study has direct the church towards what the focus should be for the preacher on how to, effectively reach the Postmodernist world.

The Uniqueness of the Message

Preaching the Word of God is unique and different from every other form of speech. The people said that Christ's words were not the same as the scribes and the Pharisees. In fact Mark 1:22 tells us the people were astonished at Christ's doctrine: "for he taught them as one that that had authority, and not as the scribes." That is because preaching the Word of God contains the Spirit of God, where his presence is known and felt. Anything less is merely a speech. To preach Christ is to preach the history of Christ, and to preach Christ as a present reality is to preach Christ in his fullness, with the Holy Spirit as our guide.

The Gospel is central theologically. Christ is presented in the New Testament as the fulfillment of the Old Testament and proclaims Himself to be the goal of all the purposes of God. This is the focus of preaching. The Gospels contain the message that God has revealed himself in the flesh and that he came to this earth and dwelled among us. The Gospels contain not just the words of love for people, but also the demonstrated love of Christ at Calvary. Christ is humanity's means of contact with the truth of God, and proclaiming the Good News lets listeners hear who God is. This means they should not hear the opinions of men, but the perspective of God. Preachers are to be the proclaimers of God's Word and the listeners should receive nothing less. Luke 24:27 records that Christ is the focus of all scripture: "And beginning with Moses and all the Prophets, he explained to them what was said in all the Scriptures concerning himself."

Regarding the effects of preaching the gospel message using rhetoric and apologetics, Stott says in his book, *The Art of Preaching in the Twentieth Century: Between Two Worlds,* that preaching has an unbroken tradition of nearly twenty centuries in the church.[141]

Stott contends in *Biblical Preaching* that messages must be attractive because, "preaching is never stale or dull or academic, but fresh and pungent with the living authority of God."[142] "In the Greco-Roman world of the first century A.D. the preaching philosopher, employing the finely polished Greek rhetoric, was not an unfamiliar figure" adds John Broadus in *On the Preparation and Delivery of Sermons.*[143]

The main thrust of this book has been explaining that preaching to the postmodernist should incorporate rhetoric for stylistic purposes and apologetics for substantive content. Preachers need the Holy Spirit as they present the Gospel message while delighting the soul with the way the message is presented. Biblical scholars, such as Craddock and Lischer (as quoted in Hogan and Reid), "agree that there is a fundamental relationship between the art of preaching and the art of speaking (rhetoric)."[144] Cicero said (as quoted by Herrick) that "Rhetoric's great power is useful only when tempered by great wisdom."[145]

Apologetics is also necessary because it brings about reason and logic for the postmodernists, who view the Christian faith as unproven and defying the laws of reason and logic. Many religious institutions and churches, in fact, teach that knowledge, reason, and logic are hostile to the Christian faith, even though they are God-given attributes. Even though the church may not be comfortable with those attributes, the postmodernists are very comfortable with them.

Matthew 22:37 commands us as believers to "love the Lord thy God with all thy heart, and with all thy soul, and with all thy mind." The mind should not be neglected. God created the mind. Unfortunately, some have treated wisdom as if it is hostile toward God. Wisdom, however, advances knowledge, which, in turn, gives understanding. What a person believes is important!

The point is that the heart, mind, and soul, all need to be reached. Rhetoric and apologetics are the ways we capture the listener to accept the preaching as the truth, and the Holy Spirit penetrates the soul. Rhetoric touches the emotions of a person while apologetics reaches the individual through reason and logic. Peter Kreeft and Ronald K. Tacelli say in their *Handbook of Christian Apologetics* that "Even the most perfect argument does not move people as much as emotion, desire, and concrete experience. Most of us know that our heart is the center, not our head."[146] Unfortunately, preaching is often viewed as boring, and the thought of many in the church is just "to take your medicine."

Most medicines years ago never tasted good, but they would help an ailing body. Sermons were often considered the same: "They may not taste great but they're good for you." This should not be the case. Preaching should be attention-grabbing and effective. George E. Sweazey says in his book *Preaching the Good News* that "Communication research tries to discover the methods that will achieve these results. Advertisers study motivation; educators study the learning process; lawyers study persuasion; politicians are eager for new insights on how attitudes can be changed. Preachers need to know about all of these. The various purposes of preaching require a wide gamut of special communication skills."[147]

Model For Communicating With Postmodernists

Kenton Anderson has introduced a model for communicating with postmodernists. This model approaches the postmodernist all-inclusively, where you speak to the individual on every level, as this book has shown.

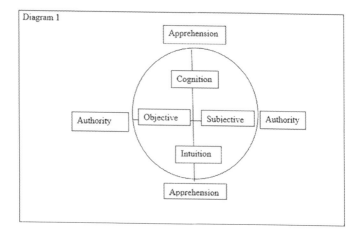

Diagram 1

Subjective Authority

According to Anderson, authority is divided into subjective and objective. Subjective authority occurs whenever the listener perceives a matter to be true, even though it may not be. It is a perception or experience that validates the matter as true. Whether God exists is probably the most fundamental and important question humanity faces. When I write in terms of theism, (i.e., a belief in God or gods,) I refer to Christian theism, as Thiessen, et al. do, "that the belief in one personal God, both immanent and transcendent, who exists in three personal distinctions, known respectively as Father, Son, and Holy Spirit.... God has revealed Himself and that man is capable of apprehending this revelation."[148] The reason lies in Romans 1:19-20, "because that which is known about God is evident within them; for God made it evident to them. For since the creation of the world His invisible attributes, His eternal power and divine nature, have been clearly seen, being understood through what has been made, so that they are without excuse."

The postmodernist can be shown the truth through natural theology. This is a way to bring in what is physically seen in the Truth of God. Davis says, "Offering theistic proofs is an aspect of an enterprise that is called natural theology. Natural theology is the attempt to reach sound conclusions about (among other things) the existence and nature of God based on human reasoning alone. Natural theology uses such human cognitive faculties as experience, memory, introspection, deductive reasoning, inductive reasoning, (which I will understand as including probabilistic and analogical reasoning), and inference to the best explanation. It is to be contrasted with revealed theology, which is the attempt to reach sound conclusions about the existence and nature of God (among other things) based on statements that are said to be revealed by God or events that supposedly reveal something of God."[149]

Objective Authority

Objective authority is a matter that is firmly established, such as the fact that the earth is round and the sun is hot. The preacher should be a dependable source of objective authority. Perhaps every listener does not believe in God. However, when the message is presented by a preacher of good moral character who knows the subject matter thoroughly, the postmodernist will listen.

Listeners will never accept the preacher's message unless they accept the messenger as a dependable source. That is why the character of the speaker is an important aspect of being an objective authority on the subject being presented. Sweazey says, "Aristotle said that the *ethos*, the character of the speaker has most to do with the results of public speech because we believe good men more fully and readily accepted than others."[150] He added, "It is not true, as some writers assume in their treaties on rhetoric, that the personal goodness revealed by the speaker contributes nothing to his power of persuasion; on the contrary, his character may be called the most effective means of persuasion he possesses."[151] Aristotle realized this statement is true for all listeners. It was not necessarily a moral judgment but an observation of every man.

The orator is to be knowledgeable of his or her topic. It is difficult to persuade anyone about anything if you are not knowledgeable about your subject. Audiences realize when someone is unprepared and will identify that in the preacher. This is why apologetics should be used in a sermon, to show the knowledge base of the preacher and the message. Further, if a Christian is uncertain of his or her biblical position, he or she will not be able to hold his or her ground and have little hope of convincing anyone else, so apologetics is paramount when preaching.

Cognition Apprehension

Apprehension means to take hold of the message and make it part of your life. It is divided into two categories: cognition and intuition. Cognition apprehension is directed at the mind, dealing with reason and logic. Apologetics, by itself, is substantive and factual because many people require substantive and factual information. Postmodernists are convinced that religion is irrational. Apologetics refutes that belief with a reasoned defense. It offers compelling explanations for the Christian belief. The role of the Holy Spirit is to use our arguments to convince the unbeliever of the truth of Christianity and to edify the believers. When a person presents reasons for his or her faith, he or she is not working apart from or against the Holy Spirit.

To return to a point mentioned earlier, it is unbalanced and unscriptural to simply preach the Gospel without addressing the unbeliever's questions or objections. Give an answer to everyone who asks! First, it is unbalanced because it assumes the Holy Spirit works only through preaching. However, we can work through rational arguments, as well. The preacher must speak to the head as well as the heart. If an unbeliever objects that the Bible is unreliable because it is a translation of a translation, the answer is not to tell him or her to get right with God. The answer is to explain that we have excellent manuscripts of the Bible in the original Greek and Hebrew languages and then talk to that person about the way to salvation. Second, it is unscriptural to refuse to reason with an unbeliever, as we read in Acts 17:2-3, 17; 19:8; and 28:23. William Lane Craig in his book, *Reasonable Faith; Christian Truth and Apologetics 3rd Edition*, urges us to "Look at Paul. It is Paul's standard procedure to present reasons for the truth of the Gospel and so defend the faith."[152]

Earlier I discussed the history of apologetics in the lives of Christians and how it has been met with assorted reactions, often ridicule and adversity. Many Christians believe reason is in conflict or in opposition to faith. Kreeft and Tacelli contend in their book, *Handbook of Christian Apologetics*, that "reason is a friend, not an enemy, to faith"[153]

They also say: "The fact that apologetics is not nearly as important as love does not mean it is not very, very important. The fact that health is not as important as wisdom does not mean health is not very important-much more important than money, for instance…. Further, another deeper reason why some people scorn apologetics reasoning is that they decide whether to believe or not with their hearts much more than with their heads. Even the most perfect argument does not move people as much as emotion, desire and concrete experience. Most of us know that our heart is our center, not our head. But apologetics gets to the heart through the head. The head is important precisely because it is a gate to the heart. We can love only what we know."[154]

In Matthew 13:12 Jesus said to the people "unto every one that shall be given, and he shall have abundance; but from him that hath not shall be taken away even that which he hath." This makes it clear how important it is to know the Word of God. William Barclay says in *The Promise of the Spirit*, "The more a man studies Scripture with every help which scholarship can give him, the more the Holy Spirit will shine upon the pages of Scripture, and illuminate them, so that there will emerge from them flashes of truth which he has hither to never seen…. The harder a man works and thinks and studies to find out the meaning of the word of God, the more the Holy Spirit can reveal to him."[155]

According to John M. Frame, author of *Apologetics to the Glory of God*: "Apologetics and preaching are not two different things. Both are attempts to reach unbelievers for Christ. Preaching is apologetic because it aims at persuasion. Apologetics is preaching because it presents the gospel, aiming at conversation and sanctification. However, the two activities do have different perspectives or emphasis. Apologetics emphasizes the aspect of rational persuasion, while preaching emphasizes the seeking of Godly change in people's lives. However, if rational persuasion is a persuasion of the heart, then it is the same thing as Godly change. God is the persuader-converter, but he works through our testimony.[156]

Apologetics not only helps the church reach postmodernists

who have little to no biblical background, but it also presents regular churchgoers with a reason to trust and have faith in God's Word. Christians also need sound reasoning as well as something biblically solid to stand on.

Many years ago, I met a man who spent many years in the Pentecostal church. For one reason or another, he left the Pentecostal church and became a Jehovah's Witness. The Pentecostals and the Jehovah's Witness doctrines are figuratively miles apart from one another. The only reasonable explanation for this far-reaching radical change is because the man could not have had a solid Christian biblical foundation and no relationship with the Lord Jesus Christ. How tragic! What had he been listening to on Sunday mornings over the years? We are warned in Ephesians 4:14, "That we henceforth be no more children, tossed to and fro, and carried about with every wind of doctrine, by the sleight of men, and cunning craftiness, whereby they lie in wait to deceive."

Apologetics goes further by reaching out to the postmodernist with the belief that the universe is of divine design because it is common for postmodernists to reject the Bible. Most scientists would overwhelmingly agree that we live in a finely tuned universe. However, to go further, the universe does not just have a designer; it has an Intelligent Designer. Not only has the Creator made the universe from nothing, but he also continues to sustain the universe.

Apologetics is used to show the full side of defending the faith. Craig et al. believe that we need a "defensive apologetic to answer the charge that to believe in God without evidence is irrational, as well as an offensive apologetic to answer the charge that to believe in God without evidence is irrational…offensive apologetics to try to persuade those who doubt Christianity."[157]

Intuition Apprehension

The intuition apprehension is the heart, which touches the emotions. This is where rhetoric comes into play. Postmodernists need to be persuaded. Phillips Brooks defined preaching as "truth through personality."[158] A speaker is often viewed as deceptive and not to be trusted, but, in fact, good rhetorical skills will touch the emotions. Combining the Word of God with rhetoric and an explanation of the logic of the Word of God brings about a powerful combination that will move the postmodernist toward the Truth.

Through using this model to support my study, one can see that preaching should be delivered using an all-inclusive method because we are not all the same when receiving messages. Apologetics, by itself, is substantive and factual but if not delivered effectively it may come across as dry and flat. Many people require substantive and factual information. Many postmodernists are convinced that any religion that holds an "absolute truth" is irrational. Apologetics refutes that belief with a reasoned defense through compelling explanations for the Christian belief, while rhetoric delivers the message that will appeal to the emotions. Streett says "There are two avenues of approaching the will: the intellect and the emotions. A man can be moved to action if his mind can be convinced that the action is reasonable, and if his heart can be convinced that the action is necessary. You must, therefore, bring your hearer to the point where he says, I can be saved (mind). I must be saved (emotions). I will be saved (will)."[159]

Notes

139. Barna Group, American Christians Do Not Believe that Satan or the Holy Spirit Exist, last modified April 10, 2009, accessed December 5, 2013, https://www.barna.org/barna-update/article/12-faithspirituality/260-most-american-christians-do-not-believe-that-satan-or-the-holy-spirit-exis#.UwlNTjYo5D8.

140. Nathan Creitz. Against Preaching: Preaching In A Media-Saturated Culture, accessed December 10, 2013, http://nathancreitz.net/preaching-ina-media-saturated-culture/

141. John R.W. Stott. The Art of Preaching in the Twentieth Century: Between Two Worlds (Grand Rapids, MI: William B. Eerdmans Publishing Company, 1982), 10.

142. John Stott. Biblical Preaching Today (Grand Rapids, MI: William B. Eerdmans Publishing Company, 1961), 30.

143. John A. Broadus. On the Preparation and Delivery of Sermons (San Francisco: CA, Harper San Francisco, 1979), 1.

144. Hogan & Reid, 13.

145. Herrick, 102.

146. Peter Kreeft & Ronald K. Tacelli. Handbook of Christian Apologetics (Downers Grove, IL: InterVarsity Press, 1994), 21.

147. George E. Sweazey. Preaching the Good News (Englewood Cliffs, NJ: Prentice-Hall, INC., 1976), 53-54.

148. Thiessen, et al., 49.

149. Stephen T. Davis. God, Reason & Theistic Proofs (Grand Rapids, MI: W.M. B. Eerdmans publishing Company, 1997), vii.

150. Sweazey, 51.

151. Ibid.

152. William Lane Craig. Reasonable Faith; Christian Truth and Apologetics 3rd Edition (Wheaton, IL, Cross Way Books, 2008), 56.

153. Kreeft & Tacelli, 21.

154. Ibid.

155. Barclay, 98.

156. John M. Frame. Apologetics to the Glory of God (Phillipsburg, NJ: P & R Publishing, 1994), 17.

157. William Lane Craig, et al. The Five Views on Apologetics (Grand Rapids, MI: Zondervan, 2000), 69.

158. Accessed 01-02-2014, http://www.preaching.com/resources/past-masters/ 11566820

159. Streett, 159.

CHAPTER 8

Remember, The Gospel is Good News!

$\mathfrak{P}$reaching the scriptural message of the Gospel is good news and preaching is at the very center of Christianity. Sweazey says "The low times in the history of the Church have invariably been those when preaching was neglected."[160]. Many in the church do not realize the benefits of Christianity. If the church does not realize this, how will we convincingly convey and persuade the message to others? Craig stated, "since almost all intelligent adult Christians are bombarded throughout their education and adult life with multifarious defeaters for Christianity, it seems that for a great many, if not most, people, rational argument and evidence will be indispensable to the sustenance of their faith."[161].

Faith without evidence, of some sort, will appear to be irrational to postmodernists. I am not suggesting we find evidence to base our claim, but theistic proofs are often apparent. Also, I do not propose that apologetic arguments by themselves can bring a person to faith in Christ, but theistic proofs could certainly move a person in that direction. The classical theistic arguments, after all, attempt to prove the existence of God. Thiessen says in his *Introductory Lectures in Systematic Theology* "God has endowed man with reason and the thing that is wrong is not the use of it, but the abuse of it."[162]. That too can be said of rhetoric. There is nothing wrong with rhetoric in and of itself or the power of persuasion when used to the Glory of God.

The intellectuals of the world often view the Christian faith as foolish. Christians have an uphill battle against the accusations of being intolerant, self-righteous, bigoted, and narrow-minded. Christianity has often struggled to gain respect in the western world, and it is often the brunt of many jokes. So, not all people will be reached with the method of effective preaching. For example, in John 18:4-7, we read the story of Christ standing in the garden of Gethsemane. "So Jesus, knowing all the things that were coming upon Him, went forth and said to them, 'Whom do you seek?' They answered Him, 'Jesus the Nazarene.' He said to them, 'I am He.'" And Judas also, who was betraying Him, was standing with them. So when He said to them, "I am He," they drew back and fell to the ground." The Words of Christ were filled with such power that they were knocked to the ground. They failed to realize that Jesus of Nazareth was not an ordinary man. They did not realize the obvious. A person could witness one of the greatest of miracles and be so determined to resist the Holy Spirit that they hardened their hearts so that there is nothing that will penetrate their heart.

Throughout this book, I have referred to biblical or expository preaching. The only thing that nourishes the people of God is the Word of God. We all have heard something we have said taken out of context; often times God is taken out of context, as well. The world of real estate is all about location, location, location. Scripture is about context, context, context. Expository preaching honors the text and feeds the souls of those who hear. Textual preaching is vital to the spiritual health of all believers, and the preacher should "touch the broken heart with the healing hand like that of the Divine Physician,"[163] as Andrew Watterson Blackwood says in *Expository Preaching for Today*.

The objection throughout the years has been that expository sermons are dull. The argument is it is not the sermon that is tiresome but often the presentation, and that is where rhetoric comes into play. In the classical Greek era, scholars believed in heartfelt arguments. As Herrick says, "emotion and reason were not separated in Greek thought, but were viewed as aspects of the same crucially important undertaking—thinking things through and arriving at rational judgments."[164]

Some preachers' presentations are dull, but that does not mean the divinely inspired scriptures are. Some highly educated theologians have incredible biblical, historical, and archeological knowledge, yet have neglected the homiletical aspects of preaching. It is not enough to have a strong knowledge of scripture, but a vibrant presentation is essential to the outcome. That is why rhetoric is vital to preaching. The presentation is vital to the impact of the sermon. That does not mean that we sacrifice style for substance, but the preacher has a divine purpose of pointing the way to heaven and proclaim the biblical message, in order that humanity be saved. Streett says, "The Word of God used by the Holy Spirit convicts men of their sins (Hebrews 4:12), enlightens their minds (Psalm 119:130), generates faith (Romans 10:17), and produces salvation (2 Timothy 3:15)."[165]

Although I have separated this book into preaching, rhetoric, and apologetics for the postmodernist audience, every sermon must be biblical, persuasive, and substantive. Preaching in and of itself is what God the Father sent his Son to do, as Luke 4:18 says: "The Spirit of the Lord is upon me, because he hath anointed me to preach the gospel to the poor; he hath sent me to heal the brokenhearted, to preach deliverance to the captives, and recovering of sight to the blind, to set at liberty them that are."

Stott says in *Between Two Worlds: The Challenge of Preaching Today* that "Professor Wingren sees human beings as 'defeated,' but preaching, conquered,' in bondage to sin, guilt and death, and sees preaching as the means of their liberation. It belongs to the nature of the office of preaching that has its place in the battle between God and the Devil."[166] He continues, "The word of the preacher is an attack on the prison in which man is held."[167] Not everyone will be reached, but we should take every opportunity to try, for 2 Peter 3:9 says "For it is God's will that none shall perish." With the help of the Spirit of the Lord, we too should be determined to reach as many as we can.

Postmodernism, as I have discussed, is a view of pessimism

and hopelessness. So postmodernists live in sadness and darkness. Authentic preaching of the Word of God, however, both proclaims and defends the gospel message, a message of certain hope for the world. The task of preaching in this twenty-first-century postmodern world is to preach where Christ is exalted and where the ultimate goal is to lead people to full spiritual maturity in Him. Closing with Herrick, "It is the duty, then, of the interpreter and teacher of Holy Scripture, the defender of the true faith and the opponent of error, both to teach what is right and to refute what is wrong, and in the performance of this task to conciliate the hostile, to rouse the careless, and to tell the ignorant both what is occurring at present and what is probable in the future."[168]

Notes

160. Sweazey, 7.
161. The Five Views on Apologetics, 33.
162. Thiessen, 43.
163. Andrew Watterson Blackwood. Expository Preaching for Today (New York, NY: Abingdon-Cokesbury Press, 1953), 17.
164. Herrick, 83.
165. Streett, 158.
166. John R.W. Stott. Between Two Worlds: The Challenge of Preaching Today (Grand Rapids, MI: William B. Eerdmans Publishing Company, 1982), 95.
167. Ibid., 124.
168. Herrick, 212.

Bibliography

This is a list of publications that are cited in the book as well as those that are not cited, but are nonetheless valuable for further research on the topic of reaching postmodernists for Christ.

Adams, Jay E. *Preaching with Purpose*. Grand Rapids, MI: Zondervan, 1982.

Adam, Peter. *Speaking God's Words: A Practical Theology of Preaching*. Vancouver, BC: Regent College Publishing, 2004.

Anderson, Kenton C. *Preaching with Conviction*. Grand Rapids, MI: Kregel Publications, 2001.

Aquinas, Thomas. *Aquinas Summa Theological*. Notre Dame, IN: Ave Maria Press., 1989.

Barclay, William. *The Promise of the Spirit*. Philadelphia, PA: The Westminster Press, 1960.

Barna Group, *American Christians Do Not Believe that Satan or the Holy Spirit Exist*, last modified April 10, 2009, accessed December 5, 2013, https://www.barna.org/barna-update/article/12-faithspirituality/260-most-american-christians-do-not-believe-that-satan-or-the-holy-spirit-exis#.UwlNTjYo5D8.

Bartholomew, C., R. Parry, and A. West. *The Futures of Evangelicalism: Issues and Prospects*. Grand Rapids, MI: Kregel Publications, 2003.

Blackwood, Andrew Watterson. *Expository Preaching for Today*. New York, NY: Abingdon-Cokesbury Press, 1953.

Boa, Kenneth & Bowman, Robert M. *Faith has its Reasons Integrative Approach Defending Christian Faith*. Downers Grove, IL: InterVarsity Press, 2005.

Broadus, John A. *On the Preparation and Delivery of Sermons*. San Francisco, CA: Harper San Francisco, 1979.

Bush, L. Russ. *Classical Readings in Christian Apologetics: A.D. 100-1800*. Grand Rapids, MI: Academia Books, 1983.

Chapell, Bryan. *Christ-Centered Preaching*. Grand Rapids, MI: Baker Academic, 2005.

Christian Post, accessed April 15, 2014, http://www.christianpost.com/news/southern-baptist-pastors-hope-to-revitalize-hundreds-of-churches-in-decline-117912/.

Cohen, Gary G. *Biblical Decision Making, Intelligent Design and Creation*. Eugene, OR: Resource Publishers, 2006.

Corbett, Edward P., J. Corbet & Robert J. Connors. *Classical Rhetoric For the Modern Student (4th ed.)*. New York, NY: Oxford University Press, 1999.

Cowan, Steven B. *Five Views of Apologetics*. Grand Rapids, MI: Zondervan Publishing House, 2000.

Craig, William Lane, Habermas, Gary R., Frame, John M., Cark, Kelly James, & Feinberg, Paul D. *Five Views on Apologetics*. Grand Rapids, MI: Zondervan, 2000.

Davis, Stephen T. *God, Reason and Theistic Proofs*. Grand Rapids, MI: WM B. Eerdmans Publishing Company, 1997.

De Romilly, Jacqueline. *Magic and Rhetoric in Ancient Greece*. Cambridge, MA: Harvard University Press, 1975.

De Vres, Henri. *The Work of the Holy Spirit*. Grand Rapids, MI: WM. B. Eerdmans Publishing Company, 1956.

Dodd, C.H. *The Apostolic Preaching*. New York, NY: Harper & Row Publishers, 1964.

Dulles, Avery Cardinal. *A History of Apologetics*. San Francisco, CA: Ignatius Press, 1999.

Dunn-Wilson, David. *A Mirror for the Church*. Grand Rapids, MI: William B. Eerdmans Publishing Company, 2005.

Edwards Jr., O.C. *A History of Preaching*. Nashville, TN: Abingdon Press, 2004.

Fogarty, Stephen. Web Journals, "Toward a Pentecostal Hermeneutic," http://webjournals.ac.edu.au/journals/PCBC/vol5-no2/toward-a-pentecostal-hermeneutic (assessed April 14, 2013).

Frame, John M. *Apologetics to the Glory of God*. Phillipsburg, NJ: P & R Publishing, 1994.

Fuhrmann, Manfred. *Cicero and the Roman Republic*. trans. W.E. Yuill. New York, NY: Oxford University Press, 1992.

Geisler, Norman. L. and Frank Turek. *I Don't have Enough Faith to be an Atheist*. Wheaton, IL: Crossway Books, 2004.

Gibson, Scott M. *Preaching to a Shifting Culture*. Grand Rapids, MI: Baker Books, 2004.

Goldworthy, Graeme. *Preaching the Whole Bible as Christian Scripture*. Grand Rapids, MI: William B. Eerdmans Publishing Company, 2000.

Greidanus, Sidney. *Preaching Christ from the Old Testament*. Grand Rapids, MI: William B. Eerdmans Publishing Company, 1999.

Grenz, S. J. *A Primer on Postmodernism*. Grand Rapids, MI: William B. Eerdmans Publishing Company, 1996.

Grudem, Wayne. *Systematic Theology*. Grand Rapids, MI: Zondervan Publishing House, 1994.

Gundry, Stanley N. & Steven B. Cowan. *Five Views on Apologetics*. Grand Rapids, MI: Zondervan, 2000.

Helmbold, W.C. *Plato: Gorgias*. New York, NY: Classic Books America, 2009.

Herrick, James A. *The History and Theory of Rhetoric*. Boston, MA: Pearson, 2009.

Hiebert, D. Edmond. *Mark: A Portrait of the Servant*. Chicago, IL: Moody Press, 1974.

Hoekema, Anthony A. *Created in God's Image*. Grand Rapids, MI: William B. Eerdmans Publishing Company, 1986.

Hogan, Lucy Lind & Reid, Robert. *Connecting with the Congregation*. Nashville, TN: Abingdon Press, 1999.

Johnston, Graham. *Preaching to a Postmodern World*. Grand Rapids, MI: Baker Books, 2001.

Kemper, D. A. *Effective Preaching*. Philadelphia, PA: The Westminster Press, 1985.

Kreeft, Peter & Tacelli, Ronald K. *Handbook of Christian Apologetics.* Downers Grove, IL: InterVarsity Press, 1994.

Kuyper, A. *The Work of the Holy Spirit.* Grand Rapids, MI: WM. B. Eerdmans Publishing Co., 1900.

Lenski, R.C.H. *Commentary on the New Testament: the Interpretation of the Epistle to the Hebrews and of the Epistle of James.* Peabody, MA: Hendrickson Publishing House, 1998.

Lischer, Richard. *The Preacher King.* New York, NY: Oxford Press, 1995.

Lischer, Richard. *Theories of Preaching: Selected Readings in the Homiletically Tradition.* Durham, NC: The Labyrinth Press, 1987.

_____ *A Theology of Preaching.* Eugene, OR: Wipf and Stock Publishers, 1992.

Lloyd-Jones, D. Martyn. *Preaching and Preachers.* Grand Rapids, MI: Zondervan Publishing House, 1972.

Locke, John. *Essay on Human Understanding.* Mineola, NY: Dover Publications, 1959.

Loscalzo, Craig A. *Evangelistic Preaching that Connects.* Downers Grove, IL: InterVarsity Press, 1995.

_____ *Apologetic Preaching: Proclaiming Christ to a Postmodern World.* Downers Grove, IL: InterVarsity Press, Downers Grove, IL, 2000.

Mathewson, Steven D. *The Art of Preaching Old Testament Narrative.* Ada, MI: Baker Academic, 2002.

May, James M. *Trials of Character: The Eloquence of Ciceronian Ethos.* Chapel Hill, NC: University of North Carolina Press, 1988.

McQuilkin, Robertson. *Understanding and Applying the Bible.* Chicago, IL: Moody Press, 1992.

Miller, Perry. *The New England Mind, The Seventeenth Century.* Cambridge, MA: Harvard University Press, 1983.

Mohler, R. A. Jr. *He is not Silent: Preaching in a Postmodern World.* Chicago, OH: Moody Publishers, 2008.

Netland, H. *Encountering Religious Pluralism.* Downers Grove, IL: IVP Academic Press, 2001.

Osborne, Grant R. *The Hermeneutical Spiral*. Downers Grove, IL: InterVarsity Press, 1991.

Perry, Marvin, Chase, Myrna, Jacob, James R., Jacob, Margaret C., & Von Laue, Theodore. *Western Civilization: Ideas, Politics, and Society*. Boston, MA: Houghton Mifflin Harcourt Publishing Company, 2009.

Pratt Jr., Richard L. *Every Thought Captive*. Phillipsburg, NJ: Presbyterian and Reform Publishing Co., 1979.

Preaching. Accessed 01-02-2014, http://www.preaching.com/resources/past-masters/11566820

Robinson, Haddon. *Preaching to Shifting Culture*. Grand Rapids, MI: Baker Books, 2004.

Ryle, J. C. *Expository Thoughts in the Gospels, vol.4*. Grand Rapids, MI: Baker Book House, 2007.

Shelley, Bruce L. *Church History in Plain Language*. Dallas, TX: Word Publishing, 1995.

Smith, R.S. *Truth and the New Kind of Christian: The Emerging Effects of Postmodernism in the Church*. Wheaton, IL: Crossway Books, 2005.

Sproul, R.C., Lindsley, Arthur, & Gerstner, John. *Classical Apologetics*. Grand Rapids, MI: Zondervan Publishing House, 1984.

Stanford Encyclopedia of Philosophy. http://plato.stanford.edu/entries/fideism

Stewart, James S. *Heralds of God*. New York, NY: Charles Scribner's Sons, 1946.

Streett, R. Alan. *The Effective Invitation*. Grand Rapids, MI: Kregel Academic & Professional, 1984.

Stott, John R.W. *Biblical Preaching Today*. Grand Rapids, MI: William B. Eerdmans Publishing Company, 1961.

_____*Between Two Worlds: The Art of Preaching in the Twentieth Century*. Downers Grove, IL: InterVarsity Press, 1982.

_____*Evangelical Truth: A Personal Plea for Unity, Integrity, & Faithfulness*. Downers Grove, IL: InterVarsity Press, 1999.

Swears, Thomas R. *Preaching to the Head and Heart*. Nashville, TN: Abingdon Press, 2000.

Sweazey, George E. *Preaching the Good News*. Englewood, NJ: Prentice-Hall, Inc., 1976.

The Preachers Forum. *Exploring Rhetoric and Rhetorical Criticism*.

www. http://preachersforum.org/?page_id=80 (accessed 01-12-2014).

Thiessen, Henry Clarence. *Introductory Lectures in Systematic Theology*. Grand Rapids, MI: WM. B. Eerdmans Publishing Company, 1949.

Unger, Merrill. *The Modern Preacher, Principles of Expository Preaching*. Grand Rapids, MI: Zondervan, 1955.

Vanhoozer, Kevin J. *Is There a Meaning in This Text?* Grand Rapids, MI: Zondervan, 1998.

Vickers, Brian. *In Defense of Rhetoric*. New York, NY: Oxford University Press, 1988.

Wilson, David-Dunn. *A Mirror for the Church*. Grand Rapids, MI: William B. Eerdmans Publishing Company, 2005.

Wilson, Paul Scott. *A Concise History of Preaching*. Nashville, TN: Abingdon Press, 1992.

Zimmerman, Paul A. *Darwin, Evolution, and Creation*. Saint Louis, MO: Concordia Publishing House, 1959.

William Barclay, *The Promise of the Spirit* (Philadelphia, PA: The Westminister Press, 1960), 12.

'

Printed in the United States
By Bookmasters